A CHRONICLE OF A TRIBE

WORLDWIDE GOTHIC

NATASHA SCHARF

Published in 2011 by
INDEPENDENT MUSIC PRESS

Independent Music Press is an imprint
of I.M.P. Publishing Ltd

This Edition © Independent Music Press

Worldwide Gothic: A Chronicle of a Tribe
by Natasha Scharf

British Library Cataloguing-in-Publication Data.
A catalogue for this book is available from
The British Library.

ISBN 978-1-906191-19-1
Cover design by Fresh Lemon

 INDEPENDENT MUSIC PRESS

P.O. Box 69, Church Stretton, Shropshire SY6 6WZ
Visit us on the web at: www.impbooks.com

Simon Hinkler in the 1985 line-up of The Sisters Of Mercy ... and a lot of dry ice!
© Pat Hawkes-Reed

Worldwide Gothic

A Chronicle of a Tribe

by Natasha Scharf

Independent Music Press

ACKNOWLEDGEMENTS

The author would like to extend her gratitude to everyone who helped with photos, interviews, research and contacts for her book.

Special thanks must go to: Martin Roach, CE Tuke, Zena Scharf, Michael and Andi Johnson, Christian Riou, Simona and Jason, Matthew North, Mick Mercer and www.mickmercer.com, Taya Uddin, Lady Amaranth, Larysa K, Thomas Abresche, Ralf Epke, Per-Ake Warn, Stephane Lord, Kevin Preece, Trevor Bamford, Raymond Ross, Stephen Milward and Georgia Docherty, Louis Plume, Al Pulford, Erika Grapes, Marloes Bontje, Andy Heintz, Steve Godfrey, Chris Sherrington, David McKnight, Pat Hawkes-Reed, Max Flowers, Steve Weeks, Garry Hornby, Alix Corvyn, Anne Sudworth, Ryan Swift, Neville Cope, Stefanie Valtre, James Thompson, Rosi Uwins, Rachael Huntington, Steve Cox, AndromedaX, Maurice Grunbaum, Starkall, Szelevényi Gellért, Kate Seagroat, Ash and Michelle Ghoulmore, Daniela Barría Segovia, Farzana Fiaz, Cadavre Exquis, Ruby Soho, Lauryn Malott, Daniel Dodecahedron, Si Denbigh, Trotwood, Somi Arian, Hilla Bernstein, Hans Miniar Jónsson, Yair Abelson, Tracey Gibson, Chizzy, Adam Sagir, Jerry Ewing, Malcolm Dome, Jonathan Selzer, Ester Segarra, Tish and Snooky, Geoff Kayson, cats and cake, all the PRs and record labels who helped... and anyone else I might have accidentally left off!

Cover Credits:
Model: Lady Amaranth
Photography: Taya Uddin
Corset: Larysa K
Jewellery: Alchemy Gothic

This book is dedicated to the memory of Fred Scharf

ONCE UPON A GOTH...

Without punk, there would be no goth and without glam, there would be no punk. What started as a semi-political and slightly pretentious youth culture in the UK has since developed into an image-orientated and highly creative subculture that has assimilated a variety of musical and fashion influences as it has spread it wings and cast mysterious shadows across the world.

The secret of goth's longevity is not only its constant evolution but its appeal to the darker sides of the human psyche. This book dips a pointy-toed boot into the bottomless whirlpool that is the worldwide gothic scene.

THE BIRTH

Monday, 20 September 1976, London, England.
A bunch of snotty-nosed teens with a penchant for swearing were about to
headline one of the most memorable shows in punk history. The Sex Pistols
had been placed right at the centre of a new musical movement with a big
attitude problem that was sweeping across Cool Britannia, claiming to wipe
away all those aging MOR rock bands and Eurovision kitschness with anarchy
and safety pins. Hordes of sweaty youngsters were cramming themselves into
the tiny venue on Oxford Circus that night eager to catch a glimpse of this
crazy new band whose music was unlike anything they had heard before.
Inside the 100 Club, the Punk Special was so busy that even the walls seemed
to be perspiring but few realised that today would also be the birth of
something else that was just as exciting. One of the opening acts was called
Siouxsie And The Banshees – they were so new they hadn't any songs of their
own yet nor even a proper line-up. Instead they performed a wailing mash-up
of covers including a version of 'The Lord's Prayer' taking musical cues from
Roxy Music, T-Rex and the Velvet Underground. Although no one realised at
the time, they would become one of the best known faces of a subculture
known simply as 'Goth' that would draw influences from not only punk but
also glam rock, cinema, literature and philosophy.

"[Back then] the only two women I could think of in rock 'n' roll who
I loved were Suzi Quatro and Patti Smith and they were both American,"
remembers Bromley punk rocker Michelle Archer, who was first in the queue
for the 100 Club show. "Suddenly there's this British 'ice queen' on stage …
she came over as über-cool to us 16-year-old girls and boys. It also seemed it
was the first time a member of the audience [had taken] to the stage and it was
a female to boot …"

Empowered by the "hot goddess" she'd seen on stage, the teenager would
go on to form her own band the VDUs at Ravensbourne Art College, which
would then merge into Brigandage just a few years later. She explains: "[We
were] a reaction against the leather-jacketed machismo 'Oi' bands and
skinhead factions, trying to inject life and colour into culture where downers
and heroin were now the norm."

Punk thrived in British popular youth culture until roughly around 1979 by
which time it had seemingly all but vanished. The Sex Pistols died with Sid
Vicious – Johnny Rotten was part of a new, much artier band called Public
Image Limited – and the media vultures were hungry for something new.
"I remember there was a distinct shift in the music [around this time]," recalls
webzine editor and former London goth gig promoter Michael Johnson.

"It wasn't all thrashy, shouty, straight-up punk any more. New bands were coming through who'd obviously copped a healthy dose of punk attitude but, equally obviously, were doing something different. These bands were cinematic and melodramatic, arch and arty, tribal and weird, deliberately trying to push things out there. *Something new is happening*, I thought. I didn't quite know what it was – nobody knew at that stage – but I knew that I liked it.

"Siouxsie And the Banshees were already there," he continues. "Siouxsie herself would disagree with me, I'm sure, but I always felt the Banshees never quite fitted in with punk. They were always too cerebral to mix it with the riff 'n' shout brigade. They were much more compatible with the emerging goth aesthetic. PIL's *Metal Box* album was [also] massively influential in creating this new aesthetic [but] nobody ever mentions PIL in this context."

And so a string of new bands started to emerge alongside Brigandage. Killing Joke, Adam And The Ants, UK Decay, Gloria Mundi, Ausgang, Blood And Roses – they were all just a little too thoughtful to fit in with all the teenage angst and arrogance that seemed to surround punk and it was time for a new name to define them. Post-punk summed it up rather neatly although eventually this new movement would become known as 'goth' – an identifier that would help push the sound and image in an even more melancholic and striking direction. Likewise punk had also given birth to the industrial genre – an experimental, beatless sound that at first seems to have little in common with what would eventually become known as goth, yet eventually elements of it would be brought under its dark umbrella with cross-over acts like Coventry's Attrition.

In 1978 in the North-West, just outside Manchester, a group of punk lads changed their band name from Warsaw to Joy Division. Their music followed a more melancholic direction and their debut album *Unknown Pleasures* received promising reviews in the music press, who picked up on the dark, empty sound that perfectly reflected the bleak landscape against which it was written. A year later in Crawley, three musicians calling themselves The Cure had also released their debut, *Three Imaginary Boys* through Polydor Records. It had taken them three years to get snapped up by the label and at the time they were referred to as a "post-punk" act, often photographed in jeans and biker jackets with very ordinary hair and no make-up. Legendary broadcaster DJ John Peel offered the band some radio sessions to help raise their profile and a few years later, they would be visually quite unrecognisable from their earlier more casual image.

Siouxsie Sioux in Chicago © Pat Hawkes-Reed

Just three months later and geographically somewhere in between in Northamptonshire, a four-piece by the name of Bauhaus released their first single. It was called 'Bela Lugosi's Dead' and was a sinister tribute to the horror movie actor who was most famous for playing Dracula. The song clocked in at over nine minutes and was later featured in the 1983 vampire film *The Hunger*, in which Bauhaus themselves had a cameo role as a band playing in a nightclub. Frontman Peter Murphy later described himself as "[the] founding father of the Gothic movement" on his official website. These are just a few of the most memorable bands who were doing something different during a time of musical purgatory.

This wasn't the first time the undead had crept into popular music though. The Damned had been doing it since 1976 when they burst onto the scene with their debut seven-inch 'New Rose', which is now regarded as the first punk single despite certain band members having a somewhat gothic aesthetic. Frontman and horror fan Dave Vanian favoured black eye make-up and a vampiric cloak on stage – while off-stage he dug graves for a living. There was a definite movement of some kind starting to emerge, defined by an edgy, glam-meets-punk-rock kind of sound and a slightly theatrical image but it would take a few more years before it would really catch on.

Meanwhile, against the backdrop of terrorism, Ireland was also busy creating its own version of this nascent post-punk scene. The Virgin Prunes provided quite a contrast to the riotous anthems of The Undertones, Boomtown Rats and Stiff Little Fingers while exuding a much artier vibe than the more subdued rock of their mates U2. Their live shows frequently featured a visual attack of cross-dressing and foodstuffs and they eventually found a more welcoming audience across the sea in England.

The common ingredients of a very visual movement were now starting to appear: black clothes, pale skin, introverted lyrics and melancholic songs all performed with the energy of punk and the theatre of glam rock. Gradually audiences started to pick up on this look, which was easy to recreate with second-hand clothing, theatrical supplies and a bit of creativity. This was surely a trend but post-punk as a monicker just wasn't quite cutting it anymore so it was time to go back to the drawing board.

It seemed there were two distinct groups starting to emerge: there were those who took the spirit of punk to try to change things and those who were heading in a much darker, maybe even morbid direction. In February 1981, *Sounds* magazine printed an article that seemed to hit the nail right on the coffin lid. "We'd gone to this big gothic cathedral in Cologne," Steven 'Abbo' Abbot from Luton-based UK Decay remembers, "and we were looking at photos of things that were decayed and I thought that just summed up our music. We were still punk but there was something decaying and gothic about our sound. A few days later, we were in Belgium doing the *Sounds* interview

The Damned circa 1983 © Mick Mercer (www.mickmercer.com)

Olli Wisdom and Jonny Slut from Specimen © Mick Mercer

The early years of London's Batcave Club © Mick Mercer

Nik Fiend meets Nick Cave in Birmingham 1984
© Mick Mercer

with [journalist] Steve Keaton and I came up with something that had a local feel: Punk Gothique. I thought it suggested a bit of mystery but didn't really give it much more thought."

GOTHIC INVASION

It took until May for *NME* to pick up on the phrase and that was in a posthumous review of Joy Division's second album *Closer*, released a short while after frontman Ian Curtis took his own life on the eve of the band's US tour. Even then the magazine still needed some convincing as it tried to rebrand the movement again with the 'positive punk' tag in February 1983. It was Michelle Brigandage's then-boyfriend Richard North from Blood And Roses who was talked into writing the piece that mentions Southern Death Cult, Danse Society, Virgin Prunes and Specimen among others. Michelle Brigandage explains. "It wasn't his choice of name [and] he didn't want to do it but was told they'd get someone from outside of the scene to write it if he didn't…" But that wasn't the name that eventually stuck.

"By the time we got back to the UK," Abbo remembers, "people started to ask us more about 'goth'. They wanted to know which other bands were gothic but the bands themselves wanted to disown the tag!" He continues: "I remember Steven Severin [Siouxsie And The Banshees] calling me Mr Goth after the interview! The media had been looking for a name to describe what had been going on and once there was a name, it could be put into this box."

The Banshees' fourth offering *JuJu* with its sinister sounds and horror theme was quickly picked up in 1981 as being the new sound of gothic by the music press but in *Siouxsie And The Banshees: The Authorised Biography*, Steven Severin recalls the band had actually used the adjective to describe their second album, *Join Hands* three years earlier.

The gothic aesthetic and those bands it was associated with existed long before the term was incorporated as a subcultural one and although from the outside, it might have looked a bit like a pantomime, life on the inside was quite different. Sex Gang Children seemed inspired by everything the word 'gothic' represented and embraced it – vocalist Andi Sexgang was even referred to as 'Count Visgoth' behind-the-scenes and Southern Death Cult's Ian Astbury's public mocking of Sex Gang Children's fans as "goths" helped give further relevance to the word. Alien Sex Fiend's Nik Fiend remembers a split scene: "In 1982, Siouxsie And The Banshees were [still] firmly under the 'punk' label. To be fair to them, musically they were outside of punk… but there was no label for all of the different types of music that were surfacing. Back then 'the scene' was any freak – be that multi-coloured hair or big hair, fishnets, lace, leather… Everyone knew each other or they were into some other freak weirdo bands."

It was those 'freak weirdo bands' with their different sounds and looks that dragged what would later become known as goth in a more literal direction via London's club-land. Although a lot of gothic ideas were already floating around in the ether it took until the summer of 1982 for The Batcave club to be founded by Olli Wisdom and Jon Klein from the band Specimen (later referred to as The Specimen). It was there that Nik Fiend, who occasionally worked on the door, took inspiration to form his own band Alien Sex Fiend. Born out of necessity as the alternative clubbing scene had dissolved with the closure of Blitz – the night frequently credited with spawning the New Romantic movement – it was originally held in Soho but relocated several times throughout its existence. The Batcave became a safe haven for the elaborately dressed, although its original playlists leaned heavily towards the '70s glam rock side of things, with the occasional bit of reggae made popular by punk DJ-cum-film maker Don Letts. "The biggest surprise for me was when they played the Sex Pistols the first night we went and people left the dancefloor!" Mrs Fiend remembers. "That was a first and a definite sign for us that something was changing musically!"

As more bands emerged with a similar dark sound and look, the club's set-list was adapted to include them, and live shows by up-and-coming bands like Sexbeat, Alien Sex Fiend and Specimen were frequently hosted. The 'positive punk' label gradually faded without a trace and the Batcave is now recognised as being the UK's very first goth night. Its punters, famous or otherwise, were frequently snapped by newspapers and style bibles. Naturally photographers would focus on those with a wackier or more extreme dark wardrobe, which in turn came to define the gothic look. This pool of creativity didn't go unnoticed by Batcave regular Nick Cave, then fronting The Birthday Party. Originally part of Australia's post-punk scene, the band's use of heavy feedback and screeching vocals gave them a more avant-garde feel than their Aussie peers. Their sound and dangerous edge seemed to fit far better in London, where they chose to record their manic and possibly prophetic single 'Release The Bats' in 1981.

"The word 'gothic' was always meant to be ambiguous," explains UK Decay's Abbo. "It was philosophical and dark but when the media just started using it, I felt like we'd been misunderstood. That's why we split up. The later bands made it more like a fashion but we'd always worn black clothes just because they didn't show up the dirt on tour and made us stand out on stage. To us, graveyards and zombies were used as metaphors rather than in the literal sense and when later goth bands such as The Sisters Of Mercy and The Mission came along, they just felt like a parody."

And so the purists argued that 'goth' now stood for something quite different.

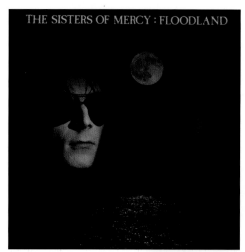

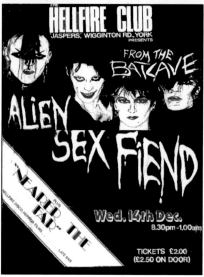

Flyer from York's Hellfire Club,
December 1983

But it was those bands – along with Siouxsie And The Banshees, The Cure, The Cult and The Fields Of The Nephilim – who really helped raise its profile and catapult it from the underground to popular culture by the mid-1980s, not just in the UK but across the globe. Their music and striking looks helped redefine what the media and fans alike understood by the term 'gothic' and they have since become universally recognised templates for what was soon to erupt into an actual subculture.

DEMONS OF THE NORTH

While all this was taking place, something similarly dark and interesting was bubbling up in the North of England. Inspired by the wealth of exciting bands like Gang Of Four that were rising from punk's ashes, promoter John F Keenan decided to host a festival in Leeds to promote all this new music. Futurama was billed as "The World's First Science Fiction Music Festival" and took place in 1979 at the Queens Hall, featuring Joy Division supporting Public Image Limited. Naturally there were some punks who felt it had turned something underground into a commercial venture but it certainly encouraged a far bigger audience to embrace this new musical scene and Futurama continued to showcase new alternative bands for another ten years.

Leeds' connection with dark music continued with further events in the area, including the infamous F-Club, where Andrew Eldritch is said to have formed The Sisters Of Mercy but it was a support band who had one of the biggest impacts on the area. "I put Nightmares In Wax on with The Cramps in March 1980," recalls Keenan. "Their entourage turned up wearing all black and I remember Pete Burns [lead singer] wearing jewellery made out of chicken bones. He had these black contact lenses in that covered his whole eye – he said they were dog contact lenses that his optician had adapted. No one else looked like him at that time." Their stage act involved a vast amount of dry ice, which Keenan believes inspired Andrew Eldritch and within a year, black clothing had replaced rockabilly denims as the uniform of choice among young followers of alternative music in Leeds even though –as Abbohas pointed out – many of the bands were wearing it simply because it made them stand out on stage and didn't show up the dirt! A short while later the band changed their name to Dead Or Alive and brought in former punk guitarist Wayne Hussey, who Eldritch would later recruit for The Sisters.

The Northern scene began to grow rapidly with The Sisters Of Mercy, Southern Death Cult (later Death Cult and then just The Cult), Siiiii, Danse Society, Skeletal Family, Red Lorry Yellow Lorry and March Violets all scoring varying degrees of fame along the way. Si from The March Violets ran his own music nights at the university under the banner of 'Music for the Masses' and

15

Flesh For Lulu
© Mick Mercer (www.mickmercer.com)

promoted shows at the Tartan Bar. In April 1983, a new alternative night called The Hellfire Club was founded in York which eventually pursued a more gothic path and lay a stake in being the first northern club to use cobwebs as decoration – something that became their trademark. The Futurama festival that came a few months later had a decidedly gothic flavour with Killing Joke, Death Cult and Flesh For Lulu all on the bill and a local newspaper review at the time referred to Leeds as "gothic city". But neither the northern nor the southern alternative scenes could have guessed that what they were part of was about to become embraced by the mainstream.

If the late '70s and early '80s had encouraged such alternative activity in the UK, there was something just as era-defining happening out on the continent. While not every country had embraced the punk movement as whole-heartedly as the Brits, there was a cultural shift that welcomed these new and exciting sounds. There the post-punk scene had earned itself the moniker 'new wave' with the bleak gothic style referred to as 'dark wave' (or 'darkwave') and in France it was frequently called 'cold wave'. Initially these tags were applied to bands coming out of the UK but quickly local acts started to form. In France, these included the shoegazery Breath Of Life, the electronic Clair Obscur, the Virgin Prunes-inspired Neva and the sexy electro-industrial Die

Form who had been around since 1978 – French goths became known as either 'gothique', 'Curist' or even 'Crow', long before the graphic novel or the movie of the same name. Notably one of the first French bands to inspire the movement was the Stooges-inspired punk group Stinky Toys who had played on the same bill as Siouxsie And The Banshees at that 100 Club Punk Special back in 1976. "Most of the bands were part of the French alternative rock scene," explains French punk Vincent Villalon aka Vx who is now part of the band Punish Yourself. "It was a development of the punk movement with a real DIY ethos – completely independent from any corporate business and it had an experimental or arty attitude… Bands like Marquis de Sade, Orchestre Rouge and Indochine (now a very popular French band) were part of a larger scene, which attracted a very mixed crowd. In a way, it was closer to the UK anarcho-punk spirit

Jonas A from The Leather Nun
© Per-Ake Warn

than to anything [now referred to as] goth. Cold wave wasn't really influenced by the UK Batcave movement but it did share a lot of common references, from David Bowie to Suicide and obviously Joy Division."

In Belgium, bands like the punkier Red Zebra and synthpoppers The Neon Judgement came from the early '80s new wave scene, which seemed quite different from what had been happening in the UK, although Red Zebra's sound would gradually develop into something much darker. Belgium's leaning towards the more electronic end of the spectrum would pose particular relevance towards the end of the decade as its strong electronic scene would cross over with a new dark movement calling itself EBM.

The UK post-punk scene actually had more of an effect on Spain – by 1981 Madrid had been kissed by goth and its influence was all around, especially in the music of Décima Víctima notably one of the most prolific post-punk bands in what became known as the 'movida española'. They were inspired not only by psychedelic '60s bands like The Doors and The Velvet Underground but also the new sounds of Joy Division, Bauhaus, The Cure and Killing Joke. Although their existence was short, it paved the way for other bands such as Alaska and the synth-poppy Fangoria to satiate the tastes of this new movement.

In Portugal's capital city of Lisbon, post-punk was thriving at a dark-spot calling itself Rock House, which held regular events. Often under the banner of Vanguarda – the Portuguese version of the new wave movement – bands like Morituri (who opened for Lords Of The New Church in 1988), Ocaso Épico, Negra Troop and GNR made up the compact Portuguese dark alternative scene. They would later be joined by Linha Geral in 1989, who both looked and sounded like a Portuguese version of Joy Division. Further south in Greece, local punk bands started following a darker path, again inspired by the likes of The Birthday Party, Bauhaus and, in 1985, The Cure who captivated the crowd at Rock In Athens. Metro Decay and South Of No North were two darkwave bands that emerged from that underground scene in the '80s.

Further north in Iceland, the anarcho-punk band KUKL, featuring quirky vocalist Bjork, turned over a gothic page with their experimental post-punk debut *The Eye* released through Crass Records in 1984. Their noticeable change of style came as a shock to fans and a few years later they disbanded and followed a more indie path with the Sugarcubes. Bjork's favourite dark atmospheric rock band HAM also steered their sound in a different direction and became more of a metal band.

Whereas labels like gothic and post-punk hemmed British bands into a very specific sound, 'darkwave' felt more relaxed and it was partly because of this that more electronic genres could be assimilated with the scene as time went on. Industrial music, which had its roots with the German experimental-electro bands Kraftwerk and DAF, and darker synth-pop were successfully crossed over, explaining why a number of seemingly disparate styles of music have since become associated with the gothic genre. This merger of styles is particularly interesting as a number of the early UK goth bands were big fans of electronic music – Bauhaus had spent the early part of their tours listening to the New York electronic band Suicide while UK Decay alternated between DAF and the classical sounds of Wagner.

Germany's version of new wave had already started to have an effect on the nearby Netherlands by the early 1980s. Clan Of Xymox's Ronny Moorings remembers: "Where I lived in Nijmegen, the German Wave was very influential with bands like Einsturzenden Neubauten [but] the market was definitely dominated by English bands. I remember the first record I made on my own label, a Dutch reviewer did not understand the synthesizers and called them magic boxes!"

In many parts of Sweden, punk's trace was shaped into the popular hair metal and glam scene but an underground movement called 'Svartrock' had also begun to emerge. Just like the word 'goth', it was an ambiguous term that meant both dark rock and black coat, which became a staple item of the gothic wardrobe, and several bands such as Dansdepartementet and The Leather Nun (who both audibly and visually perhaps inspired The Sisters' Andrew Eldritch) became associated with the genre.

In nearby Finland, a gothic movement was slowly developing from all the punk and post-punk music that was coming through on import. It was like a breath of warm air to teenagers in the bleak and cold country and it didn't take long for a small local scene to emerge. Finnish rock and punk music traditionally follows minor scales and carries a strong sense of melancholy so it was appropriate that goth's sombre mood should eventually become integrated with popular music there. Bands like the Bauhaus-inspired and very underground Syyskuu (featuring bassist Archzie who would later join gothic rockers The 69 Eyes), Musta Paraati and Liikkuvat Lapset became prolific on Finland's gothic underground in those early years. "Musta Paraati played in the biggest clubs around Finland and appeared in magazines that usually wrote only about bands in the top charts," remembers Finnish punk Kimmo Kuokka, aka DJ Ximmo. The band broke up after their second release citing internal conflicts but this was most definitely not the end of Finland's flirtation with dark music.

Despite South Africa's well-documented poverty and racial tensions, goth found its way there too in the early '80s, sharing space with the local alternative scene that incorporated punk and metal. It took its musical melancholy and dark fashion cues from the UK's emerging goth scene as well as surrounding scenes like New Romantic and rock which was filtered through the music. "In both the punk and goth scenes from the '80s I remember very few, if any, American influences in the bands we listened to or our style of dress," remembers Raymond Ross from Ankst. Two of the key local acts from the early scene were No Friends Of Harry and The Gathering. No Friends formed in Johannesburg around 1986 with a sound that took inspiration from Skeletal Family, The Sisters Of Mercy and Nick Cave but promptly veered off to the more rock end of the alternative spectrum. The Gathering, not to be confused with the Dutch band of the same name, had a short-lived career with a sound reminiscent of The Fields Of The Nephilim.

Rozz Williams circa 1984
© Mick Mercer (www.mickmercer.com)

Patricia Morrison in The Gun Club © Pat Hawkes-Reed

Christian Death in 1984, taken shortly before they performed at London's Batcave © Mick Mercer

Skinny Puppy Nivek Ogre on stage
in Ontario circa 1984
© Lauryn Malott

Poison Ivy from The Cramps in the early '80s © Pat Hawkes-Reed

Both bands helped bring a greater awareness of the scene even though it wasn't quite enough to keep it afloat as a separate movement. What probably didn't help was that back in the days of apartheid, South African goths were treated with the same disdain as the black community. "In this country [if you looked different] you got put in the back of a fucking police van and beaten…" Ankst keyboardist David Van Tonder told Radio Nightbreed during the South African broadcast edition of the *Side Show* in early 2011.

Over in the USA, things couldn't have been more different. Malcolm McLaren might have used The Ramones and the New York Dolls as templates for the Sex Pistols but the East Coast scene was a world away from what had been going on in London. Many UK punks had been spurred into action by the country's political unrest and constant striking but American punks were more driven by the American Dream of believing anything was possible. The early garage rock of bands like The Stooges and Patti Smith had already covered political territory while The Velvet Underground had crossed over with experimental sounds. Punk gave way to the short-lived 'New York No Wave' scene that would go on to impact greatly on '90s grunge (although two of its bands would later impact upon goth). Teenage Jesus and the Jerks featured vocalist Lydia Lunch who would later go onto collaborate with Nick Cave among others and then there was the highly experimental Swans. Their chaotic sound borrowed ideas like detuned guitars and alternating time-signatures from the post-punk movement and with Jarboe's often distorted vocals, they would become highly influential on the industrial movement, which would later be cross-referenced to goth. They, and avant-garde Californian musician and vocalist Diamanda Galás, would also go on to have a great deal of influence on what would eventually be referred to as extreme music which would later cross parts with the European goth scene. But none of this could really compare to the psychobilly riot that called itself The Cramps. Frequently playing at the legendary downtown dive CBGBs, the band disembowelled rock 'n' roll and the blues, dressing them up in voodoo references and trailer trash leopard print. Perhaps not instantly recognisable as a goth band, they quickly became part of the dark underground movement with their unpredictable live shows, which often ended up with singer Lux Interior in various stages of undress. Goth never happened in the same way there as it had over in the UK and in 1980 they relocated to LA and became part of a different scene but their music and striking looks would continue to have a huge impact on the goth movement even after several decades.

Over on the West Coast, punk's politics reigned with hardcore bands like The Germs, The Adolescents and Black Flag (singer Henry Rollins was originally part of Washington's punk movement). But the UK scene stirred something in disillusioned LA glam punk Patrik Mata. "It was John Lydon's manifesto of anyone being able to make music and express themselves through

The Cramps © Mick Mercer (www.mickmercer.com)

just being themselves that led me to roam the Hollywood wilderness for anyone who felt the same way," he remembers. "But [back in 1977] nobody from the then LA punk scene would play with me." He was eventually introduced to Darby Crash from The Germs and recruited as a guitarist for his solo project – Crash had recently returned from London with a new mohawk and some Indian feathers so seemed to be on the same page. Mata's involvement didn't last very long so after a few months he took the opportunity to begin developing a band of his own. "The punk rock scene at that time just became so contrived to me," he says. "I wanted to hear and maybe even bring to the scene a band influenced by Bowie's Berlin Trilogy [*Low*, *Heroes* and *Lodger*], Kraftwerk, PIL, Killing Joke and Joy Division – bands in this mindset with this kind of music." What he came up with was Kommunity Fuck – or Kommunity FK for short.

DEATH ROCK

There was still a very real feeling that changes could be made and barriers broken down but maybe not through metaphors as UK Decay had been hoping. "We went to America and got asked about gothic there," Abbo remembers. "We were touring with Dead Kennedys and Black Flag but people didn't understand our music, nevermind I was talking pretentious crap about Nietzsche and darkness!" But by the early '80s, touring bands like Killing Joke, Public Image Limited and UK Decay themselves had paved the way for a different sound. Kommunity FK bagged a support slot with Killing Joke at the famous rock venue Whisky A-Go-Go even though the crowd didn't yet appreciate what they were about and they were greeted by jeers and toilet paper missiles. But Mata wasn't disillusioned because he could see what was beginning to pan out: "I began to notice other darker bands starting to get it together... [all-girl band featuring Dinah Cancer from 45 Grave] Castration Squad came about earlier [although] they didn't really stay for long ... And then there was Rozz Williams' Christian Death..." The LA punk scene was about to give birth to a very strange creature ... and it had nothing whatsoever to do with the British concept of positive punk.

"There was so much going on because of the freedom punk gave us," remembers singer and keyboard player Gitane Demone. "There was a feeling of community – shows were mixed ... you could see a performance artist like Johanna Went play with punk bands, deathrock, ska bands, pop punk, rockabilly, noise, art punk – everybody was into seeing music played with a new attitude. I know quite a few of us were impressed by what was going on in England ..."

It was here in LA that something rather curious was about to kick off.

A musician called Rozz Williams is said to have coined the term "deathrock" to describe his post-punk band Christian Death. Their sound merged punk and hard rock with a much darker, more sinister edge that was augmented by Williams' own morbid poetry. Artier than what UK Decay had referred to as Punk Gothique, Christian Death pushed the boundaries of LA post-punk with their death-orientated imagery and disturbing sounds. Mata has always been a big fan of his work. "I love Rozz and have the utmost deep respect for him," he says. "He brought performance art to his onstage performances as he explored this art form – it was a great thing for deathrock. It was original [and still] important to this day for deathrock bands."

The original Christian Death line-up featured guitarist Rikk Agnew from punk band the Adolescents but when that line-up disintegrated in 1983 ahead of their planned European tour, Williams brought in members of Pompeii 99, the experimental rock band who were originally billed as their support act. Gitane Demone, Valor Kand and David Glass went on to record 'Catastrophe Ballet' and 'Ashes' as part of Christian Death but a rift between Kand and Williams formed shortly afterwards. This caused the two musicians to work independently of each other as Christian Death and Shadow Project (also featuring Eva O from fellow LA deathrockers Super Heroines) respectively. As the years went on, Williams' look morphed from punk to pure gothic while Gitane Demone favoured rubber and PVC fetish clothing. "Rich kids went to England and came back New Romantic," she remembers. "I wore my own mix of vintage and designer crap bought reduced and personalised by dying or shortening it… fishnets always got ripped up so you wore them anyway, [you] painted your own tees and added zips… But the majority of 'normal' citizens were shocked and disgusted by the scene… [and the police] hated the way we looked. We were harassed, followed, searched … which led to major riots at shows … I was witness to a few."

Kommunity FK's Patrik Mata remembers: "Back in 1978, I was employed by a European clothing store called Fiorucci … I had the Bowie 'wedge', dressed in black and eventually discovered white foundation at the make-up counter inside the store. It was run by a girl called Odessa and one afternoon, I asked her if she would make me up like the Pierrot character that Bowie channelled on the cover of *Scary Monsters* and I loved the way it looked. I was really skint during those times so I bought inexpensive clothing items and shoes – black patent leather shiny Oxford three-eyelet steel-capped beauties. I 'borrowed' some silver buckles from a pair of long-distance running ankle weights that a girlfriend owned and it transformed them into buckle boots. But this was before anything like this could be bought in a shop – it was makeshift street-smart fashion ingenuity!"

This new deathrock style shared some of its spooky imagery with the horror punk movement, which New Jersey band The Misfits are credited with

starting in 1976. LA bands like 45 Grave and Voodoo Church picked up on the genre a few years later, both having been originally inspired by the more experimental industrial scenes that had also dribbled out of punk. In due course, the boundaries between the two genres would become blurred and these bands would later be placed under the deathrock and then gothic rock banners.

If horror punk was the gruesome partner to British punk rock, then deathrock was goth's edgier sister. Goth had already flirted with horror's more sensual side through clothing and make-up but things were more literal in the US. Corpse-like face paint, fake blood and bandages were mixed with leather and PVC for a look that went one step beyond what even The Batcave's audience was doing at the time. Dinah Cancer from 45 Grave remembers her inspiration: "Growing up in Los Angeles in the '60s, my weekends were filled with Hammer movies. They were shown on Creature Features on Saturday nights and Sunday afternoons. I was seven when I first saw Christopher Lee but then Ingrid Pitt and Barbara Steele came on the screen and that was it; I wanted to be like them. They were the beautiful Hammer brides so for the earlier part of 45 Grave, I did the long dress and veils thing." The band's music would appropriately later appear on the soundtrack for the '80s zombie movie *Return Of The Living Dead*.

She wasn't the only one to use b-movies as her inspiration. Another band that came out of LA's punk scene was The Gun Club although their sound borrowed more from The Cramps' psychobilly style than The Misfits. Frontman Jeffrey Lee Pierce's casual style was in-keeping with the punk scene but it was bassist Patricia Morrison who caused the biggest stir with her backcombed black hair, vampish make-up and a wardrobe that looked like it belonged to Morticia Addams. Said to be inspired by actress-cum-television presenter Vampira, she stood out from the crowds even in LA.

"The Vampira look wasn't as predominant as the Siouxsie Sioux look," Patrik Mata remembers. "It's more popular now and Elvira's more cartoonish take [helped raise its profile]."

Ex-punk Drew Bernstein remembers the DIY days and used them as fuel to his LA-based cult clothing company Lip Service. "There wasn't any ready-made punk or deathrock clothing in LA around like '79, '80, '81," he explains, "so unless you were rich enough to go to England and buy some bondage pants, you made your own – I made my first pair ... I remember seeing people wearing black trench coats and then you'd DIY a shirt with fake blood spatters ... or you'd customise stuff from vintage stores. When I first became a punk, it was to rebel against the norm so when other punks came along, I went one step further by wearing more extreme clothing, like fetishwear."

He based the very first Lip Service item – a pair of leggings printed with the brand's now famous skull and dagger design – on a crucifix-adorned pair he had seen by UK company Modzart. "I thought I could do one better!" he laughs and the brand's punk and fetish-styled clothing quickly became snapped up by rock stars and the image-conscious alike as the fashion boundaries between punk, deathrock and hair metal in LA became very blurred. This blurring was soon to spread to the UK's own goth scene, which would quickly move away from basic black staples and DIY'd punk threads towards rockier leather and glammier styles of dress.

It was around the mid-1980s when the US deathrock and UK goth scenes met and where better than at the home of all things ghoulish: The Batcave. Christian Death flew over to London to perform at the club – the show had actually been rescheduled because a heavily pregnant Gitane Demone had gone into labour with her son. "I got out of hospital a week after the birth, my mother came over from California that same day, we went to the hotel and then I went to the Batcave! I remember it very well – the décor... Rozz adored the brass railing and was cabaret-ing it up, swinging his leg over it... then we played a killer set. It was a grand show [and] The Specimen were totally wonderful." And so it seemed the UK's goth and the US's deathrock scenes mutually inspired each other and this morbid marriage brought more awareness of this thing called 'goth' to the US. But there was more still to come.

Out in Canada, a varied and very underground goth scene was also flourishing; its diversity was in part due to the country's size and also the fact it spans across five different time zones. In British Columbia, Vancouver's alternative music scene in the '80s was predominantly based around benign rock in an attempt to blot out the traces left by a punk scene that included influential hardcore bands D.O.A. and the Subhumans. Record shops imported vinyl from British dark alternative bands and a new wave scene gradually began to emerge with bands like Images In Vogue and Toronto's Martha and the Muffins defining the sound. But it was another local band who made the biggest impact on the goth scene there and that was Skinny Puppy. Frontman Kevin 'Ogre' Ogilvie remembers: "[What we were doing] was kind of in revolt to what was popular at the time, which was the hair metal, glam metal stuff happening in Los Angeles ... I was into a lot of British bands [and] one that was quintessential in changing my perception of music was Joy Division."

Formed in 1982, Skinny Puppy merged post-punk with experimental industrial that had been inspired by UK band Throbbing Gristle and matched it with outspoken messages about animal cruelty and vivisection. Like Killing Joke had been doing in London, Skinny Puppy used their music to point out what was wrong with the world and later went onto cover topics such as rape, global warming and drug abuse. Their debut album *Bites* went onto spawn several gothic dancefloor hits and, although their sound grew further away from their darkwave roots as their career progressed, they remained a highly influential band in the development of goth's more electronic side.

In fact, there was something similar happening out in France with the more industrial-orientated Treponem Pal and in Switzerland with Young Gods. Both bands had all the darkness of a goth band but exhumed it through ambience and electronics in a not dissimilar way to what Skinny Puppy were doing. They preferred to refer to their music as 'post-industrialist', which spawned its own offshoots in noise, ambient and folk genres like post-apocalyptic and neofolk – all of which would later be brought together under the banner of the Schwarze Szene.

Back to Canada and in Toronto things were a little more mixed up. An early alternative subculture developed there around the early '80s that was a hybrid of punk, British New Romantic and American deathrock. Its followers were labelled 'the freaks' although some objected and later borrowed the term Blitz Kids from the London club scene. It was from this that the local goth movement was born around the late '80s.

Vampire fan Lauryn Malott remembers her teenage years in Ontario: "It wasn't called goth until like 1985, maybe '86 here. It started off with the New Romantics and sort of evolved from there – we had the music and the videos and I remember we were called the 'Scaries' or 'Morticias' in high school. But Toronto was the epicentre for sure – I can remember a trip specifically to Toronto for shopping and to get my hair done because no one where I was would cut it or dye it black for me!" With inspiration coming from the UK, not only from the more traditional Siouxsie And The Banshees/The Cure end of things but also through the safer dark pop of polka-dotted duo Strawberry Switchblade, Ontario's goth scene matched the archetypal look with mostly imported music and horror authors like Anne Rice and Montréal-based Nancy Kilpatrick. Although as with the Vancouver scene, it was electronic-industrial music that would have more of an impact later on.

With activity taking place on both sides of the Atlantic, there was one British man who played a rather significant role in the rising popularity of the bands that are now referred to as goth and that was broadcaster John Peel.

Through playing them on his Radio 1 show and recording sessions that were frequently released as standalone albums, he brought many an underground band into the homes of listeners up and down the country. Journalist Mick Mercer had also been championing the gothic cause first through *Panache*, then through *ZigZag* magazine and later in *Melody Maker*. As this new dark style developed, many teenagers (and Robert Smith!) initially mimicked the striking styles of punky icons like Siouxsie Sioux and Specimen's Jonny Slut. Fishnets, lace, PVC, stiletto boots, huge hair and heavy make-up were popular with those wishing to make an impact although this shocking look was usually toned down in more rural areas. But as the music changed around the mid-'80s, so did the dress and goth was starting to emerge from its smaller 'alternative scene' and become embraced by more mainstream popular culture. It wasn't just in reflection of the changing faces at the time – The Sisters, The Mission, Fields Of The Nephilm – but also with reference to new interpretations of the word 'gothic' that had arisen simply

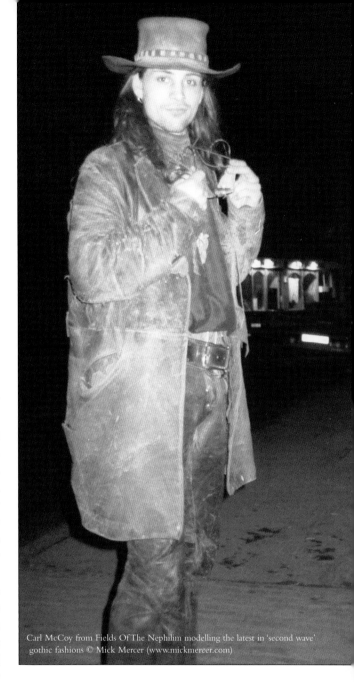

Carl McCoy from Fields Of The Nephilim modelling the latest in 'second wave' gothic fashions © Mick Mercer (www.mickmercer.com)

through this new scene earning itself, and indeed accepting, a name. Cowboy hats and leathers were popular but frilled New Romantic and pirate shirts were also starting to make an appearance, as they were twisted into the gothic urchin and dandy image by Brigandage. This look quickly became integrated with popular '80s fashion as more commercial bands like Duran Duran and Spandau Ballet adopted a toned down and 'safer', more acceptable version. Black was still the key colour with glamorous velvet evening wear and Madonna-style lace basques starting to creep into women's wardrobes.

Dave Vanian from The Damned does vampire chic © Mick Mercer

The very cuts and luxury fabrics used in '80s clothing came to define the now more glamorous gothic look, which was teamed with the heavy make-up and big hair of the decade. Punk band The Damned, now without Captain Sensible, further pushed the gothic vampire image on their *Phantasmagoria* album and single 'Eloise' although their music sat firmly within the realms of psyche-delic pop-punk.

America has long capitalised on Halloween as an excuse for a good old celebration, what with apple-bobbing and trick-or-treating. Although its festivities bear little resemblance to Mexico's more religious Day Of The Dead, its cultural knowledge of dress-up and ghoulish décor made it much easier for goth to sneak into the mainstream. Shows like The *Munsters* and *The Addams family* – whose characters were based on Universal Studios' key horror stars – had been popular favourites since the 1960s and it was there that vampires went from cult with underground movies like *Near Dark* (which portrayed them as brutal killers) to mainstream with the Brat Pack flick *The Lost Boys* in 1987. In British cinema, vamps had always been sexy but in the US they were now also cool and word was spreading to the UK. The Banshees, Specimen and The Sisters had already been flung across the Atlantic to inspire and take away inspiration for themselves, which in Specimen's case involved copious amounts of a super-strength American hairspray called Aquanet to really push the boundaries of gravity with keyboard player Jonny Slut's trademark huge hair. The Cure's creepy 'Lulluby' video was wrapped in Halloween cobwebs and those "candy-striped legs" that soon became a popular gothic wardrobe staple and former Gun Club bassist Patricia Morrison was invited to join The Sisters Of Mercy just before the release of their seminal gothic rock album *Floodland*. Her darkly sexy look, complete with corsets and black lace gloves, did not go

4AD signees Xmal Deutschland in 1984. Joan Geoffroy © Mick Mercer (www.mickmercer.com)

unnoticed as she replaced Siouxsie Sioux in the icon department. A year later Sioux had completely revamped her image with a Louise Brookes-style bob and a more sophisticated look for the *Peepshow* album.

"For me [our look] was quite theatrical," explains Roger O'Donnell, who joined The Cure in 1987. "I didn't think it was particularly goth. For me it was all about wearing my favourite designers and making my hair stick up." Elsewhere Fields Of The Nephilim added brown to the gothic wardrobe, albeit dusted with flour for that authentic aged look. It required bagfuls, which often got them into trouble with customs officials who refused to believe the white powder in their luggage was nothing more sinister than Home Pride.

Musically, goth was moving away from its early experimental punk sound, with some bands toning things down to ethereal levels of dream-pop or shoegazer as it had come to be known. The Cure had already adopted this approach and taken it on a progressive marathon with 1982's *Pornography*, they later built on that sound with *Disintegration* while 4AD bands Cocteau Twins (from Scotland) and Portsmouth's The Cranes wove beautiful vocals with delicate instrumentation for a sound that was out-of-this-world. Clan Of Xymox proffered a similar dreamy style albeit with electronic twinges that

33

earned them many comparisons to their peers although frontman Ronny Moorings remembers it wasn't an easy ride: "To be a foreign band, in the eyes of the British music press, was in those days pretty difficult and almost met by xenophobic remarks about [our] accents. It was also a difficult period because the mainstream really resisted change and music magazines tried to ignore certain styles of music as long as possible."

More accessible than the early discordant sounds of gothic punk, dreampop bands enjoyed some mainstream success with the folkier ethereal act All About Eve scoring a top ten hit with 'Martha's Harbour' in 1988. This was back in the days when chart positions were based around physical record sales rather than airplay so it was no mean feat but the roots of this beautiful blend of music lay in the Australian outfit Dead Can Dance. Formed in 1981 by Lisa Gerrard and British ex-pat Brendan Perry, their music was quite at odds with the MOR rock scene that Australia seemed to thrive on. They met through the 'Little Band Nights' that were frequently held as part of Melbourne's post-punk scene and semi-fictionalised in the cult movie *Dogs In Space* – a song by Perry's former band Marching Girls is even featured on the film soundtrack. Just a year after their formation, they realised that in order to progress their musical career they would have to return to Perry's birthplace London. They became part of the goth scene mostly through association as their first UK shows were performed with German proto-goths Xmal Deutschland and Welsh glam-pop goths Gene Loves Jezebel (their former band Slav Aryan featured *Zig-Zag* writer and soon-to-be vocalist with All About Eve Julianne Regan). Dead Can Dance were signed to 4AD shortly afterwards even though in their wake, Australia had started to come round to goth with both The Birthday Party and The Cure playing to sizeable audiences at Melbourne's alternative rock venue the Crystal Ballroom. Just as goth had been born from punk in the UK, so it was as well in Australia. As Aussie Z00g, who's now part of cyberpunk band Angelspit explains: "Sydney, Melbourne and Brisbane did not react to the goth scene ... they helped *build* it." Melbourne was also home to the darkwave outfit Death in the Dark, who formed at high school in 1988. They changed their name to Ikon three years later and while their influence perhaps hasn't been as great as Dead Can Dance's, they've still been a regular face on the touring circuit across the globe and have released five studio albums to date.

Dead Can Dance's ethereal style was also picked up in Italy where Ataraxia pushed the definition of "gothic" even further with their beautiful cold wave songs that were often sung in ancient languages – something the UK group Miranda Sex Garden would also go on to dabble with. Several years later founding member Katharine Blake would end up revisiting the style with her chorale group Mediaeval Baebes and found herself retaining some of her gothic audience.

Elena Fossi from Kirlian Camera © Out Of Line Records

But the rest of Italy's dark musical movement couldn't have sounded more different – the word 'goth' wasn't even applied to this scene until much later on, which perhaps explains some of its eclecticism. Spearheaded by synth-pop pioneers Kirlian Camera, whose sound became more and more sinister as the decade progressed, the Italian scene shifted more towards a definable post-punk sound by the mid-1980s but it was Rome's Carillion Del Dolore who were considered the first 'dark' band in Italy. Milan's DJ BMC remembers: "Their songs were extremely slow and despite being very charming they never made it commercially in our country nor got much of a following..." Valor from Christian Death produced their second album *Capitolo IV* which was released under their new name Petali Del Cariglione. The underground band Death in Venice formed around 1985 and Il Giardino Violetto a few years later in 1989 – all inspired by the British gothic bands that the small Italian scene was so receptive to. Their cult status and edgy music helped fuel an underground scene that would follow quite a different path by the turn of the next decade. "In the '80s there was a completely different scene [to what there is now]," explains DJ BMC. "It was the paninari [young, middle-class people who are obsessed with looking fashionable] who listened to new wave – the metallers and those who listened to darkwave were considered losers..."

In Finland, the dark underground scene was developing from those early years. In 1987, in the university city of Tampere Anne Nurmi and Jyrki Witch formed a band called Noidat. Jyrki chose to write in English and they changed their name to Two Witches. "I had just come back from the army and met Anne," the frontman remembers. "Both of us liked the same kind of music and wanted to start a band because there were no gothic bands to follow in Finland...We started recording and playing live [towards the end of the year]. Little by little we found some new friends to join the band and the story continued. But those years were really hard for gothic bands in Finland – there were only a few events per year, really hard to get gigs and only a few people in a scene."

Despite touring bands like The Sisters Of Mercy and Siouxsie And The Banshees bringing their darker sound to nearby Sweden, it wasn't until the latter part of the 1980s that a gothic scene really started to develop there. "Funhouse were one of the very first pure goth bands around," remembers Andreas Larsson, who just a few years later would go onto sign them to his label M&A MusicArt. "But their 1987 debut single 'Tormentor' was tinged with metal and it wasn't until vocalist Fredrik Täck was replaced by Mikael Korner that the sound became the more traditional '80s goth that they're now associated with."

As the scene became increasingly popular, more clubs and venues sprang up to cater for the dark masses. Larsson recalls: "Gothenburg stood out back then but where I lived in Malmö, we had regular clubs like Tin Can, with live bands

Finland's Two Witches as they were in the late '80s
© Darklands Records

... and Two Witches as they are now. © Exeria

every fortnight, and more irregular clubs like The Crypt as well. KB and Stadt Hamburg provided opportunities to see bands like The Cult, Ghostdance, The Jesus and Mary Chain and many more live. I particularly remember a night when we went to see Flesh For Lulu and then continued to an aftershow party in an occupied block of flats that was due to be torn down. The band performed an improvised extra set in front of an ecstatic audience at around four in the morning – it was a crazy night. A few days later the police stormed and cleared the block and all the buildings were torn down within a fortnight. Now there's a big state-of-the-art shopping centre in its place."

In nearby Norway, the UK's post-punk scene had already inspired the first wave of goth bands like the new wave Fra Lippo Lippi, whose music would eventually follow a poppier path, and the female-fronted Garden Of Delight (not to be confused with the German darkwave band of the same name). It would take until the next decade for a heavier, darker sound to emerge against a back-drop of a much more extreme underground music scene.

Similarly, it would be a few more years before the word 'gothic' would start to be used in Germany and even then its association would be wrapped up into something much bigger. There hadn't been much of a real punk movement there but instead the Neue Deutsche Welle, or 'wave' movement had welcomed the sounds of British bands like The Sisters Of Mercy, The Cure and Bauhaus. In West Germany, there were 'wavers' and occasionally 'ghouls' who were more interested in death and cemeteries and then there were the 'grufties'. Grufti was a slightly offensive name given to those black-clad wavers by more 'normal' people but in East Germany, it seems to have been more commonplace by the late '80s. Colloquially, it can be translated as 'old fogey' and was originally used to describe those more senior members of society who were shuffling further towards the edges of their mortal coil but goths found themselves lumped into the category simply because outsiders assumed they were obsessed with dying. Photographer Starkell remembers seeing them in his hometown in East Germany. "They dressed in black and collected bones… they really did … no kidding!" he laughs, although not entirely seriously. It seems the grufti movement took deathrock and the metaphor-heavy early UK goth scene to a very literal level. By the early 1990s, the phrase 'wave-gotik' would start to be used and Germany would gradually become home to the largest gothic movement in the world.

DEATH OF AN ERA

"Whenever the goth tag was applied from around the mid-1980s on[wards], it was used as a derogatory term as in 'useless'," explains Nik Fiend. "[Alien Sex Fiend] were called a shit band who lived in a cemetery, slept in coffins and were the stinky poor cousins."

All fashions eventually go out of favour and by the late '80s that is mostly what goth had become. Or at least that was how it seemed in the UK where it had apparently enjoyed its last dance and was being replaced by the day-glo, hyperactive beats of rave culture. The media had already begun goth baiting several years earlier and that continued well into the '90s. Those once considered cool were slated and bands brandished with the 'goth' brush were keener than ever to shake it off. The thing is, it wasn't so much goth that had become big in the 1980s, it was more that a number of bands from that scene had broken through and enjoyed chart success paving the way for their sound and look to become embraced by a wider audience. In reality, the true goth scene was always fairly compact in size even if elements of the look had filtered through into mainstream fashion and many of the bands associated with it had reaped commercial fruits both in the UK and beyond. Although they enjoyed a good level of mainstream success, The Mission's overtly-bombastic style and lyrics were often seen as a bit of a joke by many in the scene while The Cult flirted with American rock, working first with producer Rick Rubin on *Electric* and then with Bob Rock on *Sonic Temple*. Rock was credited with producing Metallica's finest album shortly afterwards as their self-titled offering was released and they became a household name. MTV's first UK broadcast in 1989 helped the career of an otherwise unknown rock band called Guns N' Roses – The Cult's former drummer Matt Sorum joined them the following year and went on to enjoy far more success than The Cult had ever experienced. Bauhaus had disintegrated in 1985 as three-quarters of the band formed the more alternative rock outfit Love And Rockets, allowing frontman Peter Murphy to get on with a more mainstream solo career, but neither project would ever have the same impact that Bauhaus did. Even Tim Bricheno from All About Eve left to join The Sisters Of Mercy and alternative rock band CNN (later renamed XCNN over legal issues) and Claytown Troupe played up to the alternative rock tag. Elsewhere, Fields Of The Nephilim burst to form many side projects including Rubicon, Saints Of Eden, Last Rites, Sensorium and Carl McCoy's more metal-orientated Nefilim. In Sweden, gothic rock bands like Stillborn and In the Colonnades were going heavier and heavier, perfecting the fusion of goth and metal even though the hybrid term wouldn't be invented for another few years. Stillborn in particular merged traditional melancholic gothic rock with heavier doom and metal elements that would be a taste of things to come in the Scandinavian scene. In Spain, the popular electronic sound was also being merged with a darker rock in the fetishy Gothic Sex, whose occasional guttural growls were a hint of things to come. Ringleaders Lord and Lady Gothic were visually steering things in a rather different direction with nefarious onstage antics that would later be

Love And Rockets at The Metro in Chicago. © Pat Hawkes Reed

incorporated into the performances of more risqué German gothic acts like Umbra Et Imago and 18 Summers.

Over in the States, where rock and metal were reigning supreme and hip-hop was starting to break through into the mainstream, Island Records had earmarked a young musician for greater things. His name was Trent Reznor and he'd written an album called *Pretty Hate Machine* under the name of Nine Inch Nails. UK producer John Fryer had been called in to mix it, having recently scored hit records on the alternative scene with Depeche Mode and Cocteau Twins. Neither mainstream rock nor commercial pop, Island wasn't entirely sure what to do with this project although they knew it had enormous potential. 'Head Like A Hole' was released as the first single and a live band of talented local musicians pieced together, while the early gigs were memorably decorated like London's Batcave

NIN's Trent Reznor © Al Pulford

club. Reznor's influences took in the early gothic sounds of Bauhaus, the more electronic futurist beats of Gary Numan and harnessed the aggression of Canadian modern industrialists Skinny Puppy, who he was chosen to support.

Skinny Puppy's Nivek Ogre remembers: "Nine Inch Nails probably did it the right way; raising through the different levels whereas we've always stayed the same … we were Leftist outsiders who never got any endorsements for anything."

Nine Inch Nails seemed to bridge a number of gaps that the punk scene had left behind. Their atmosphere and lyrical content was pure gothic, their music covered parts of the industrial base and they even had enough aggression to fit with the nu-metal scene that was on the cusp of breaking. "I have so much respect for Trent Reznor," Kommunity FK's Patrik Mata explains. "He's an innovator, an explorer [and] I *love* his music. Now this is somebody who took what he thought was 'goth' to a new place."

Reznor's sound also fitted in perfectly with the development of a new kind of industrial music that had come through Wax Trax Records, which had undeniably reached its peak in 1989 when *Pretty Hate Machine* was released. The Wax Trax label was founded around 1980, in conjunction with a music store of the same name in Chicago and went on to issue albums by influential bands such as Young Gods, KMFDM, Front 242 and Clock DVA. They were also in charge of releasing Ministry's early synth-pop singles as well as Paul Barker and Al Jourgensen's later side-projects, which steered their sound in a much heavier direction and helped develop industrial metal as a valid genre. Just as Skinny Puppy and Frontline Assembly's dark–industrial sounds had risen through Canada, it was spreading throughout the US as well. Through the varied Wax Trax roster, the label helped redefine industrial music from the early beat-less sound that Throbbing Gristle and Cabaret Voltaire had perfected into something dancier and much easier for the masses to digest. Confusingly some of the bands associated with this genre would also be referred to as 'coldwave', although the style had nothing to do with France's cold wave movement from the early '80s. However, the style complemented what Nine Inch Nails were doing and Trent Reznor would later marry the old with the new on his 1995 mini remix album *Further Down The Spiral* by bringing in industrial legends Coil and Foetus to help with remixes. Goth was being recreated, redefined and modernised although its synthesis would soon cause internal rifts and new subgenres.

Ministry at Chicago Park West, 1985 © Pat Hawkes-Reed

SYNTHESIS

If the UK media were to be believed,

by the early 1990s the goth scene was little more than a decaying lump of blackened goo. By rights this book should end here but in reality, the really exciting stuff was only just beginning to happen; a new dark rose was growing out in Europe and beyond, its petals opening further and further outwards.

But before we go any further, let's get one thing straight: the original goth movement was born from a heady mix of punk, Bowie-esque glam and the experimental garage rock of bands like The Doors and Velvet Underground. Occasionally a little horror influence would creep in, mostly from the US or as a metaphor but it never proclaimed to glorify death or dying nor did it have anything to do with the fetish or BDSM movements or even getting dressed up in historical costumes. It also had little to do with the Germanic tribe who invaded parts of the Roman Empire in the third century or even gothic architecture. The thing is, just like many negative connotations of 'gothic' were apparently forgotten during its previous 18th century revival, the origins of the goth movement were to be completely re-written by newcomers in the 1990s. In fact, some of the Norse imagery originally used by the early Gothic tribes would later become popular in some European gothic movements, likewise with copies of the medieval clothing worn during the first period of gothic architecture and the 18th and 19th century attire chosen by those who contributed to the gothic literature movement. In fact the very themes of horror, romance and melodrama – as portrayed in gothic novels and poems – became popular in this new gothic movement as it sought to develop its own identity. But of course, none of this is what the likes of *NME* and UK Decay had in mind when they plucked the g-word from the dictionary!

THE NEXT GENERATION

During the early 1990s, the various goth scenes around the world were quietly ticking over, which gave those late-comers free reign to explore the more experimental side of the genre. The stalwarts of the UK post-punk scene might have inspired bands in other countries with their spiky, often discordant sound and even striking looks but many of the early goth bands outside British shores had a very different sound compared to what's now regarded as gothic, deathrock or even post-punk. Perhaps this explains why so many have retained their cult status and are often unheard of outside their native scenes.

Loltaru from www.hairfromhell.com © Stephane Lord www.darkfairies.co.uk

France's Jacquy Bitch performing at Wave Gotik Treffen in Leipzig.
© Michael Johnson

In Greece, the Athens punk band The Flowers Of Romance were now twisting their British-inspired sound into an even darker, thornier shape – their 1995 album *Brilliant Mistakes* was even produced by The Mission's Wayne Hussey. Over in France, echoes of UK goth were being heard with darker and slightly less arty bands such as Corpus Delicti, Brotherhood of Pagans, Lucy Cries and Rosa Crux emerging. Neva frontman Jacquy Bitch launched a solo career that kept the more theatrical elements of his former band and added a much darker and more sinister edge to his music with the use of additional programming. Interestingly while Neva's sound was regarded as French post-punk at the time and has perhaps been audibly inspired by the Virgin Prunes, it doesn't sound as recognisably gothic to modern ears. British dark rock like The Mission and The Sisters had become popular there too and a new dark pop movement was also developing called 'touching pop' – the name came from Little Nemo who define it on their website as a "synthesis of the melancholic new wave side and the melodies". Taking a huge influence from The Cure, it doesn't sound too far removed from the shoegazer style. "Older musicians often dismissed this second wave [of goth], saying it was music for posers and party-fiends," remembers Vx from French band Punish Yourself. "The press was quite sarcastic about it too … but there was some really cool stuff." Little Nemo were also responsible for setting up the LivelyArt label via their New Rose imprint, which helped to further publicise this new musical style. They even signed underground British post-punk band And Also The Trees to the label and it was against this background that Punish Yourself decided to form. "We were complete misfits," Vx laughs. "The French scene was quite obsessed with The Sisters Of Mercy and The Cult at this time but we sounded like The Birthday Party, minus the blues stuff, played by ape men! Then slowly we learned how to handle a guitar and a microphone…" By 1998, France would have its very own gothic magazine called *Elegy*, which would blend the old dark culture with the new.

Over in Germany the gothic scene was moving away from the early British bands that once dominated it, creating its own style of music with classical influences and lyrics sung in the native tongue. There was nothing else like it at the time so Germany's alternative *Zillo* magazine called it Neue Deutsche Todeskunst, literally New German Death Art and for a while the name stuck. NDT bands generally used a spoken almost rapped style of lyric rather than the traditional shouted verse in wave acts like Xmal Deutschland or the sung style of The House Of Usher but ultimately it was about setting philosophical content to a darker sound. Germany's dark scene welcomed the new sounds of bands like Goethes Erben, who favoured a more electronic style that seemed to peel away the horror of Skinny Puppy's early dance beats, Das Ich, Sweet William and Artwork. These bands were all about combining music and theatre, which was frequently exhibited through make-up and clothing as well as song style and thought-provoking lyrics that fitted with Friedrich Nietzsche's theories. Goethes Erben's keyboardist at the time, who was from the US, likened them to the American 'death punks' although their style was extremely different from actual deathrock.

"There was a lot of influence coming from the classical side and lyrically, a lot coming through German baroque," explains Artwork's Jochen Schoberth, who was working as Das Ich's sound engineer. His involvement also included producing Goethes Erben's first three albums and he reveals there was a much deeper side to their lyrics. "[They were both] influenced by Günter

German Neue Deutsche Todeskunst act Das Ich © Danse Macabre Records

Abel and [other] modern philosophers… they never used any clichés but there was a feeling of being able to change things; these bands had something to say."

Other bands were emerging too. Among them were Lacrimosa, which began as a solo project and became a duo in 1993 after Anne Nurmi left Two Witches and Deine Lakaien, who had formed in 1985 as an experimental classical music project but became more immersed within this new dark movement as time went on. There was also Sopor Aeternus And The Ensemble Of Shadows who mixed in elements of dark folk, neo-classical and later medieval music, which would eventually sit side-by-side with goth in the German Schwarze Szene. This more electronic style — transplanted Brits The Legendary Pink Dots are frequently cited as an inspiration around this time — distinguished the German bands from those that had previously been part of the UK's goth scene and with many of the British gothfathers either defunct or turning to a rockier sound, goth was evolving in order to exist.

"In the '80s it was all about the British bands," explains Eric Burton from German gothic rockers Catastrophe Ballet. "But by the '90s, their sound changed so much and they didn't want to know about goth anymore so you got these new bands doing things in a German way. If you picked up a copy of *Zillo* in around 1989/1990, you'd see bands like The Mission and Cassandra Complex but a few years later, they had all disappeared [from the pages] and there was this new wave of German music. People were interested because this stuff was happening now and they didn't have to wait for the UK bands to come through with anything."

But over to the east of the country, Communism got in the way as the authoritarian governments of the time imposed strict rules in society. These regulations discouraged any form of alternative existence lest it challenge the government's policies and ideals. Music was monitored and public gatherings were discouraged in case they resulted in rioting. The Berlin Wall physically separated two parts of one city and brought with it many rules and regulations. In the East, the only way you could play in an underground band was if you were studying music and used the existing network of youth club houses to house your gigs, something that would later be utilised to build up the fanbases of many underground bands. However, there were opportunities for larger gigs if you could prove that you were pro-government or joined a political party; ironically long hair was more acceptable for men there than in the west of the country because many of the left-wing

Lacrimosa were one of the first underground gothic bands to mix symphonic metal with their sound © Angst Im Wald

terrorist groups used this as a kind of uniform. As far as clothing was concerned, black was an acceptable colour but dressing in an outlandish way would warrant accusations of homosexuality, something that was frowned upon by the Left even though it had been decriminalised a few decades earlier. As a result, the very core believes of the post-punk scene and the gothic look itself were challenged and this meant the goth scenes within Eastern Europe were very late in developing.

Towards the end of the '80s, a small goth underground scene had started to grow underground in East Germany and a rebellious hunger fuelled a black market for alternative music and culture that came from a wealthier West that was free to do as it pleased. In 1989, a goth called Michael Brunner organised a Whitsun meet-up of twenty like-minded music fans at the ruins of the Belvedere castle in Potsdam, which was just within the boundaries of East Berlin. Artwork's Jochen Schoberth travelled there from the West along with Bruno Kramm and Stefan Ackermann from Das Ich. He remembers: "Bruno heard about it from some friends and told us to come with him. At that time the border was already open so travelling was no problem and we were a little excited about what we might find."

Chris Roper dressed as Sopor Aeternus
© Simon Stacey

But by the time the trio reached the meeting point, the several hundred goths that actually turned up had been arrested by police, who assumed they were about to take part in a political demonstration. Rumour has it that the ones who managed to escape were reunited by moonlight and hid among protesters during the May Day trade union demonstration the very next day. Once the Berlin Wall came down two years later and Germany was restored to a single country, what had become two separate scenes were merged into one and in 1992, another attempt was made at a gothic meeting. This one was held in Leipzig's Eiskeller club and came to be known as Wave Gotik Treffen. Artwork were among the bands on the bill and Schobert remembers: "Nobody wanted to talk about East and West [once the wall came down]. The West Germans had the impression those from the East were poor and the East Germans said those from the West were arrogant, so everybody tried to meet without this East/West attitude. But I think it was the right time to start a festival in East Germany so early after the wall came down."

The Velvet, or Gentle Revolution which overthrew Eastern Europe's Communist regime opened the gates to the kind of freedom and creativity that had otherwise been frowned upon. A darkwave scene had already been slowly developing in what is now known as Russia with Agatha Christie forming in 1988 and the Czech Republic was just behind them in benefitting from a hive of alternative activity. Alternative music from Western Europe hit the area in the early part of the decade with the cult dark rock band XIII Stoleti. The Baltic states of Lithuania, Latvia and Estonia had always lent more towards electronic and industrial music rather than rock-based sounds but gothic rock bands still managed to filter through. Mano Juodoji Sesuo formed in 1991 and were originally compared to The Cure and The Cocteau Twins with their more shoegaze style of music. Their sound now contains stronger elements of electronic music and, along with Siela, Zalvarinis and Lauksna Lauksna, they represent the newer wave of Baltic gothic rock.

In Hungary, a shift in the political regime during the mid-1980s had opened up the borders and brought about the birth of the goth scene there a few years later – The Cure's 1989 concert in Budapest attracted more than 11,000 fans and set the wheels in motion for more to come. The first generation of gothic and deathrock bands, like Siouxsie and The Banshees, Joy Division and Christian Death, were among those that inspired this new scene and in the summer of 1991 Land Of Charon formed, taking their inspiration from Fields Of The Nephilim's dark gothic rock although they eventually moved things in a heavier direction. The post-punk Nulladik Változat also formed around the same time although the compact size of the real goth scene there means it has often become lumped in with the metal movement, with the female-fronted Without Face being one of the more popular bands at the time. Singer Julie Kiss relocated to the UK where she went on to front the progressive dark metal band To-Mera. DJ and promoter Gellért Szelevényi runs the Hungarian website Gothic.hu and the Memento Mori social network, both of which spread the dark word and keep the small scene ticking over. He explains: "Nowadays in Hungary there is one darkwave band called Autumn Twilight. Its style is 'Sisters of the Nephilim' but there are also club nights specifically for sub-genres of music like Batcave for deathrock, Nekromantika for gothic and Industrial Fusion for electronic and industrial music. The size of the scene means the mixed nights tend to work better but everyone gets along well."

Un-United kINGDOM

Necessity breeds invention and the UK's puddle of gothic goo was also starting to show some signs of life. As goth was dwindling or at least veering off in various metallic directions in the mainstream towards the end of the 1980s, a new underground movement had already started in the UK. A host of bands trickled out of the scene, mostly inspired by the sounds that had made up the earlier part of the decade. The Rose Of Avalanche, Marionettes, Every New Dead Ghost and Nosferatu were among the new breed itching to return goth to its former glory. The problem was, any impact they tried to make on mainstream media was met with mockery, which just pushed the scene even further underground where it continued to exist on a very subcultural level.

Webzine editor and former promoter Michael 'Uncle Nemesis' Johnson remembers: "The success of the Sisters and Nephilim had inspired umpteen soundalike bands. From being a glorious swirl of diversity, goth became very one-dimensional and codified. Frankly, it was difficult even for those of us who liked goth, who had been keen supporters from the beginning, to stay interested. The smaller bands kept plugging away, but it was a case of diminishing returns, really. The gigs got fewer, the goths themselves got fewer. By the early '90s goth really was clinging on by its fingernails. It never quite died, though. There's that wonderful quote by Nick Cave to the effect that after the nuclear holocaust the only survivors would be cockroaches and goths. Old Nick was on to something there ..."

Nestled among the Madchester tunes and clubs hits in the mainstream charts, there were still pockets of unexpected darkness. In 1990, perky synthpoppers Depeche Mode released the darkest album of their career up until that point. It was called *Violator* and although it wasn't 'goth' per se, there was a definite edge of gothic about it; around the same time, a new wave of shoegaze or dark indie bands also started to creep out of the woodwork including Curve, My Bloody Valentine and Lush. Along with '80s alternative rock bands such as Daisy Chainsaw (KatieJane Garside and Crispin Gray later went onto form the goth-friendly Queen Adreena), New Model Army, The Jesus And Mary Chain and The Levellers, these were among the staple listening requirements for a lot of former goths from this era who were just simply unaware that anything else was still happening. Placebo later joined this group and while a lot of this music is still played at gothic events, it's categorised as 'bands goths like' rather than gothic bands. Key producers from this period include Flood, Alan Moulder and John Fryer who would later become associated with a very specific dark sound which continues to drive a lot of gothic music to this day.

But by the mid-1990s, underground events were starting to take place again across the whole of the UK, albeit on a small scale. London in particular was a veritable hive of activity. The Marquee club, then on Charing Cross Road, ended up almost accidentally hosting a series of goth gigs when ex-punk John Banshee made good use of the venue's free Sunday 'new bands' night while he was managing a new goth band called Restoration. It wasn't long before the night became extremely popular and the venue started to charge. The Marquee was also home to a big two-day underground goth fest called Necromantic Encounters which took place on a boiling hot summer weekend in 1995. Vendemmian and Nosferatu were headliners with support coming from the likes of Suspiria, The Horatii and Die Laughing, among others.

Despite such activity, the goth scene was still very small and it was around this time that it started to find itself crossing over towards the pagan underground movement. Just as punk had borrowed religious and political symbols, often to shock, so goth did too – symbols like the ankh of life, pentagrams and the Eye Of Horus have always been as popular as crucifixes when it comes to jewellery. New Age shops became a haven for goths to buy new jewellery and more hippyish styles of clothing – their pagan principles seemed to appeal to many goths who embraced an alternative lifestyle as well as appearance. Back in London, one of the Pagan Federation's fundraisers who just happened to be a goth stumbled across a cassette by a pagan rock band from Cheltenham called The Children Of The Moon. The man in question, Mark Rimmell remembers how he found it at a car boot sale: "Back then I'd heard more than my fill of poorly recorded droning male vocals over weedy 'tish-tosh' drum machines. But The Children of the Moon was by contrast so much better than any of the other stuff I'd come across at the time. There was more light and shade to it, the songs were well constructed, and it was well produced. It took me a while before I called the number on the cassette cover … I remember being worried they may have split up." They were very much still going but had just changed their name to Incubbus Succubus.

He went to see the band on their home turf the following weekend and was so impressed that he decided he should bring them over to the London goth scene. "I saw the same faces at the Slimelight that I saw at pagan events," he remembers, "and of all the 'pagan' music I'd come across, the Inkies were by far the best. It seemed logical to bring them to London. It also helped that Tony and Candia are really lovely people, so I was more than willing to put my money where my mouth was." He and John Banshee put the band's very first London gig on at The Dome in Tufnell

The re-named Inkubbus Sukubbus performing at Whitby Gothic Weekend
© David McKnight

Park, which included support from a new London duo called Vendemmian, featuring former members of Restoration. The event was a success and would be the beginning of a long association the soon-to-be-renamed Inkubbus Sukubbus would have with the goth scene.

Naturally there were those who felt the two movements of pagan and goth shouldn't mix but in commercial terms, it made a lot of sense. Rimmell was behind a Pagan Federation fundraising event at the Marquee that also featured the pagan rock band. "The gig was not a goth gig, and not promoted as such," remembers Michael Johnson, "but because the goth/pagan crossover was in full swing at the time, and Incubus Succubus were the hottest new things in UK goth at that moment, large numbers of the crowd were goths. Add to this the Pagans who'd come out to support the cause, and the result was a sold-out venue and a great success. I think certain people didn't realise that this wasn't a typical goth gig. Batman, the Marquee's manager [who now goes by the name of Cockney Gargoyle], was so impressed with the large and enthusiastic goth crowd he started up a regular, bi-weekly Sunday night goth-slot at the venue … Even though the audiences were often very small, those Marquee goth nights played a big part in reviving the UK goth scene. For the first time there was a regular London gig-slot in a fairly major venue available for goth bands. It's not too far-fetched to say that the rise of the 1990s 'underground' goth scene started here." Conversely there were also strong Christian goth groups that emerged in the 1990s, putting paid to any suggestions that the gothic subculture might be part of the occult.

And so The Marquee events kick-started the London scene. Weekly goth nights like M:Alice Underground and Tenebrae Tarantella took over from the Batcave in Gossips – the venue underneath its original location at the Gargoyle Club/Billy's – and Slimelight became famous worldwide as London's place to be. Originally held in Westbourne Grove and known as the Kit Kat Club, it gradually morphed from squat party into a fully-fledged club night moving into a disused church in Holborn before eventually settling at its current location in Angel towards the end of the '80s. The now derelict Powerhaus in Finsbury Park became another popular venue for goth gigs at the time. In 1995 Michael Johnson adopted the name of Uncle Nemesis and, as Nemesis Promotions, became one of the capital's best-known '90s goth gig promoters.

In the East Midlands, things

Batman outside the legendary Gossips in Soho. © Stephen Milward

weren't quite as active, which inspired local goth Ryan Swift to take action and form a band called Emma Conquest. He remembers: "There were still events being put on at the larger venues, for instance Rock City in Nottingham held the odd all-nighter with the likes of Rosetta Stone, Creaming Jesus and Every New Dead Ghost on the main stage, but increasingly all the gigs were being consigned to back rooms of pubs. When we finally got round to recording a CD and began playing live in 1995, fewer decent bands seemed to be cropping up or indeed surviving, so the potential for what we thought we could achieve seemed to be becoming greater."

He adds: "I'd been having fun travelling places to see my fave bands at the time, such as The Ancestry, and would catch [the big bands at the time] like Nosferatu, The Marionettes and Rosetta Stone. It really did seem like we stood a chance of some success within the scene, as our music was being compared favourably with the likes of The Horatii and Manuskript, who were perceived as being part of the third 'tier' of popular goth bands. It all seemed very hierarchical at the time, but in a friendly way. Magazines such at *Bats & Red Velvet* [aka *BRV*] were a great source for finding new bands, and had a good readership within the UK scene, which provided more possibilities for

reaching your audience as an up-and-coming goth band. Of course, true to tradition, we always denied we were ever a goth band. But no-one was fooled for a minute …"

Following on from The Sisters and The Cult, there was quite a trend in 'denying gothness' in the '90s UK scene – it was seen as a bit of an in-joke and a true sign of being part of the gang. But while this underground goth movement was keeping itself to itself, elsewhere the legacy left by The Sisters and the Nephilm was evolving into a new subgenre that would soon come to be known as gothic metal.

53

A NEW DIRECTION

Back in the 1970s, the rock scene was the very thing that punk rebelled against – be it convoluted progressive solos or dodgy mullets, punk laughed in its face with Johnny Rotten even brandishing an 'I hate Pink Floyd' tee with pride. The 'New Wave Of British Heavy Metal' kicked in roughly around the same time as the first wave of goth but with its dirty denims and self-indulgent riffs was quite at odds with the more refined gothic style and melancholic song structure. If ever two scenes were more ill-matched then surely this was it. But London gothic punks Creaming Jesus had tried to merge the two genres towards the end of the '80s even though it was a little too aggressive and experimental for many goths. Just as the north of England had helped shape the sound of gothic rock in the late '70s and early '80s, so the area would also become responsible for helping to define a gloomy type of music that would come to be known as gothic metal, although it wouldn't cross over into the goth scene itself until the mid-1990s.

Paradise Lost in concert © Per-Ake Warn

Derived from the slow and heavy tempos of doom metal – a style originally developed by Black Sabbath – gothic metal conveys both rich atmospheres and melancholy but does so with a more extreme edge. It was the Halifax-based Paradise Lost who became the first British band associated with the genre. "We were initially an extreme death/doom band but we became unhappy with sounding like everyone else and decided to include influences from the goth music that we were into," explains guitarist and co-songwriter Greg Mackintosh. "This led to an interview with *Raw* magazine in which we were asked to sum our music up in a soundbite. We said, 'Erm, gothic metal' as we couldn't think what else to call it. This I believe was the first time anyone coined the style."

So once again it was a throwaway comment picked up by a journalist that helped define a new movement. If their 1991 album *Gothic* established their credentials as a gothic metal band, then subsequent releases made them a major inspiration for a whole host of new acts including Squid (later renamed 616 Abortions) from the UK, Portugal's Moonspell, The Gathering and After Forever, both from the Netherlands. The underground goth scene argued, and frequently still does, that this was just another name for metal but there's one thing that can't be denied. Where the underground gothic bands had failed, this new breed of gothic metal eventually roused media interest and brought fresh blood to a scene that had been written off. Ironically, it quickly became part of the German goth scene as well with Lacrimosa being one of the first NDT acts to merge metal guitars with darkwave and building it into a more symphonic structure.

"I can see how there's a logical cross-over between the two," Nightbreed's Trevor Bamford muses and he's frequently explored that connection with his own band Midnight Configuration. "Okay, if you compare say Siouxsie And The Banshees' flanging solos to Type O Negative, it's about as far away as possible but The Sisters Of Mercy developed their sound through metal so the two connect there." As if further proof were needed, The Sisters' songs have since been covered by a number of the metal bands they've inspired including Cradle Of Filth, Kreator and Sweden's Maryslim.

Paradise Lost's Greg Mackintosh adds: "We were the first gothic metal band that I am aware of but we didn't really care about that or about being pioneers; we were just doing our own thing. I don't think [goth and metal] were opposite genres – I just looked at it in terms of what emotions the music evoked and in that respect doom/death and goth were very similar. The label came after we had already established our style [but] the term 'gothic metal' has now become very broad. If you mention it to people these days they think of very commercial, romantic, flowery stuff and this is a million miles away from what we started."

Gothic metal also spread to Norway with the band Theatre Of Tragedy forming in Stavanger in 1993 against a very different back-drop. Here the more extreme black metal style dominated another corner of the underground and former Emperor musician Mortiis admits: "I can't recall a single goth band in Norway… Back in those days, I can't recall seeing a single goth anywhere. Maybe I went to the wrong clubs…"

Perhaps he did because Morendoes (previously known as Wake, also from Stavanger) were one of the Norwegian gothic bands that helped drench Theatre Of Tragedy's sound in a different kind of darkness. Like Paradise Lost, Theatre Of Tragedy originally came from the metal scene and their early music contained both death grunts and more recognisable gothic rock sounds. Theatre's founding drummer Hein Frode Hansen remembers: "When we started the band, I was listening to a lot of English gothic rock bands like The Sisters Of Mercy, March Violets, Red Lorry Yellow Lorry, Fields Of The

Nephilim and Joy Division on various compilations I'd pick up. There was something completely different about the darkness of these bands compared to the death/doom music we had been making." Equally inspired by the new breed of UK gothic doom bands like Paradise Lost, Anathema and My Dying Bride, Hansen found his band in the awkward position of being too soft for the metal scene and too heavy for the goths. Regardless they still frequented Oslo's original gothic club Gotham Nights, and not only allowed themselves to become immersed within dark underground culture but also got to know the other bands that would go on to make up the Norwegian scene.

In 1997, Morendoes founding guitarist Tommy Olsson left to join Theatre Of Tragedy and his input on the band's third album *Aégis* would later earn it the accolade of being their most gothic album. It would also become the blueprint for the plethora of female-fronted gothic metal bands that followed. "It was a natural progression," Hansen explains. "We were listening to mostly gothic rock at the time and we saw that album as homage to the greats. My drumming in particular was very much inspired by Nod Wright's from Fields Of The Nephilim although there are so many layers, you probably can't hear it."

With Olsson leaving two years later to form Elusive along with Tristania session vocalist Jan Kenneth Barkved (Olsson's brother Kenneth was also in Tristania), Theatre Of Tragedy shifted their sound once again and would do so several more times during their career, which came to a rather premature end in 2010. Their former female vocalist Liv Kristine relocated to Germany and went on to form gothic metal group Leaves' Eyes with her husband producer Alexander Krull as well as launching a more commercial solo career. Tristania and later Sirenia (formed by the former's frontman Morten Veland) were also part of this movement, which would eventually fit neatly under the umbrella of the Schwarze Szene in Germany.

Over in Finland, Two Witches and The Shadow Dance were keeping the more underground scene ticking with the former discovering new countries via tours. "The early '90s were a pretty active time in Helsinki and Tampere," remembers Santeri Ihalainen, aka DJ Santtu, citing other bands such as One Blood, Russian Love, Advanced Art, Sad Parade, Shade Factory, Dancing Golem, The Insult, [Active] Media Disease, Chaingun Operate, A-TYD. He adds: "By the mid-1990s, grunge and dance music were dominating the alternative scene so it was a bad time to be a goth; there were no shops to get clothes and records were hard to get. But if you were lucky, you could still find a goth or two lurking somewhere…"

Just as Scandinavia seemed ready for a new sound, so was Italy. In 1990, a much heavier deathrock sound was created by part-Italian/part-German band Madre Del Vizio, who have since relocated to Germany and are often referred to as bringing the European version of deathrock there. Within a few years,

Theatres Des Vampires' Sonya Scarlet
© Aural Music

a new wave of harder gothic rock acts were born with Lacuna Coil starting up in Milan, The Frozen Autumn in Turin, Theatres Des Vampires in Rome and Lacrime Di Cera in Sardinia. Theatres Des Vampires' early sound carried a much stronger black metal influence, which became more symphonic and rockier after the departure of male vocalist Lord Vampyr (aka Alessandro Nunziati) in the mid-'00s. The band flirted with controversy as singer Sonya Scarlet sometimes engaged in blood-letting on stage, which raised a few eyebrows on the goth scene – she was later encouraged to tone down her act and use fake blood although she has often defended her decision in interviews throughout the years. But it was Lacuna Coil who would find the greatest success as they were signed to Century Media Records in Europe which brought their music out to the larger UK and German audiences where it would slowly metamorphose from atmospheric darkwave to nu metal and then to dark pop.

But it wasn't just the music that was changing, it was also the tags applied to it. "There were changes," remembers Milan's DJ BMC. "New impulses and inspiration came in with an electronic wave and that brought about growth in the dark scene. The term 'gothic' was starting to be used in connection with the Scandinavian wave of gothic metal at least by the mainstream – we're talking bands like HIM, To/Die/For, Charon and For My Pain. Up until then, we'd just used the word 'gothic' to refer to architecture and artwork and The Cure, The Sisters Of Mercy – those bands – were called simply 'dark music'."

As the jigsaw pieces of this fragmented Italian dark music scene started to form a more coherent picture, so *Ascension* magazine came along in 1998 and a year after that *Ritual* magazine was born – the latter is now an official music publication with nationwide distribution. Music festivals such as Dark Day and Dark Celebration went on to provide focal meeting points for local goths along with an array of gigs and clubs to further push the genre.

A parallel gothic metal scene was running in Portugal with black metal band Moonspell gradually morphing into a much more 'gothic' shape. This was later assisted by Polish producer Waldemar Sorychta who had also been working with Lacuna Coil, Switzerland's more industrial-metal Samael and Sweden's Tiamat. All four bands were signed to Century Media by the mid-1990s, with their dark atmospherics defining a new style of European music. Yet by the time Moonspell reached 2001's *Darkness And Hope,* their sound had shifted into quite an unrecognisable shape, which would be moulded and remoulded again over the years. The more gothic rock-sounding Noctivagus followed in 1994 with Heavenwood and Phantom Vision also emerging from the same scene.

Over in the USA, goth was blossoming and its more delicate style was starting to catch on. There were Christian Death offshoots Memphisto Waltz and Shadow Project, while Faith And The Muse recreated some of the beauty that those early 4AD bands had pioneered and London After Midnight flirted with darker, whimsical imagery within their songs. Chicago – home of the influential Wax Trax! Records –became a hive of dark activity thanks to the role of DJ and promoter Scary Lady Sarah who set up American Gothic

Chicago's Scary Lady Sarah © Stephane Lord www.darkfairies.co.uk

Productions and the Nocturna dark alternative night. Goth nights were springing up elsewhere like Washington DC which had The Dollhouse, Hollywood with Bar Sinister and in Boston, Ceremony is now the area's longest-running goth club. Even the punky New York scene was turning darker with its very own version of the Batcave and more arty bands popping up like the ethereal Mors Syphilitica and quirky singer-songwriter and artist Voltaire. His satirical comic book series *Oh My Goth!* fitted in rather nicely with the growing trend towards sinister etchings that was popularised by indie companies such as Writhe And Shine and Slave Labor Graphics. Other artists included Roman Dirge and Jhonen Vasquez, whose cartoon character Invader Zim became a bit of a household name when he got his own show on the kids' cable channel Nickelodeon, while another comic called *Gloom Cookie* and British author Neil Gaiman's *Sandman* graphic novel series became essential periodicals for American goths.

In Philadelphia, DJ Patrick Rogers set up the Dancing Ferret brand which was involved in gig and club promotion and eventually became an independent record label in 1998 – The Crüxshadows were one of its most successful acts while Tapping The Vein and California's The Last Dance would also become popular. Dancing Ferret was behind the Nocturne nightclub (not to be confused with Chicago's Nocturna) and Dracula's Ball, which originally had strong ties to the popular *Vampire: The Masquerade* story-based

Goths outside the Elsinore pub at the very first Whitby Gothic Weekend in 1994
© Matthew North

role playing game, centering on modern-day vampires in a gothic world. The game fitted in well with the themes explored in Anne Rice's *Vampire Chronicles* and with the later *Blade* movie trilogy making their slightly ironic feel very popular with a number of younger goths. Dancing Ferret has since become associated with the magazine *Asleep By Dawn* and the IsoTank online music store.

Back in the UK, club nights such as Resurgence in Portsmouth, Batfink in Sheffield, and Wendyhouse in Leeds were becoming popular in the underground scene and a two-day festival was set up in North Yorkshire called the Whitby Gothic Weekend, which provided not only a meeting place but also a community to develop. Former promoter Michael Johnson explains: "The Whitby Gothic Weekend was originally about the bands coming up from the underground and the subculture that coalesced around them. Essentially, it was two big gigs by the seaside. The music was the heart of it, the entire reason the event was put together in the first place. The WGW has never been a big deal in global terms, but within the UK it gave the goth scene a major festival event that helped to pull up everything else. It gave home-grown bands a goal to work towards: their chance to get on a big stage and up their game in front of an audience far larger than they'd get anywhere else on the gig circuit. It created an event that was big enough to attract international bands to the UK – would we have seen London After Midnight, Faith And The Muse, Corpus Delicti or Switchblade Symphony touring in the UK without the presence of the WGW as a peg upon which to hang everything? Probably not ..." Other festivals sprung up like the more vampire-orientated Vamps And Tramps Ball, Sacrosanct in London and Bradford's industrial weekender Infest. The fetish-meets-goth event Carnival Of Souls in Derby also took place, and each focussed on a slightly different aspect of the genre.

This new goth scene stretched far up north to Scotland too, where Edinburgh, Glasgow and Aberdeen became the key cities. Among other nights Edinburgh had The Mission with some events held by Edgar (Edinburgh University Goth & Rock Society), Glasgow had Bedlam with occasional events being held at the Cathouse and Aberdeen had Elizium which kicked off around 1996 and was originally located in an internet café bar. Alun Hughes co-ran the night with Grant Mitchell and admits: "The early days were really heavily goth but we weren't an exceptionally serious club – for example, DJs used to forget to change records ending up in epic Fields of The Nephilim opuses! But from a core of about a dozen friends it grew into a club that was attracting more people, and we'd stay later and later until none of the goth folk were going to the [alternative night] Mudd anymore. I'd say we were playing mostly trad goth with some newer bands of the time thrown in as we found them – The Horatii, Manuskript, Die Laughing ... [it was] very much guitar-led [with lots of] white make-up and velvet." Eventually, the local student's union helped bump up Elizium's numbers but the more it expanded, the more its music policy diversified to include guitar-led industrial like Ministry and Nine Inch Nails. Within a few years it would change even more.

WORLDWIDE GOTHIC

By the mid-1990s, another wave of British goth bands had started to emerge, influenced by the more mainstream gothic rock of the '80s and supported by the underground network. All Living Fear, Libitina, Cries Of Tammuz, This Burning Effigy, Dream Disciples, Manuskript, The Horatii, Passion Play, Rome Burns, Suspiria … the new breed of gothic rock was seemingly endless and these bands quickly earned themselves the tag of 'Brit Goth' for their distinct sound that borrowed elements of dark indie with, in many cases, a pinch of knowing sarcasm. The mainstream music industry was enjoying the Brit Pop explosion with the likes of Blur and Oasis battling it out for the coveted number one position in the charts so while none of these underground bands were really poised to achieve the commercial success of their forefathers, '90s

Libitina posing in Birmingham in 1996 © Pat Hawkes-Reed

goth wasn't exactly the nadir that history books have painted it.

The bands and infrastructure for a new dawn of goth may have already been in place but the worldwide web made it so much easier for ideas to become reality. "Now that the internet is everywhere," says Michael Johnson, "it's hard to imagine what a game-changer it was when it first came along. But it changed everything. In fact, it's probably fair to say that if the internet had not come along, goths would have had to invent it. As it was, goths simply became early – very early – adopters."

Goth-exclusive chatrooms and news groups were quickly founded and the term net.goth became common-use. The quiet adoption was mostly down to the simple fact that a large number of goths during this period were either students or working in IT so had this new information super-highway right at their fingertips. It also had the added bonus of doubling up as a free marketing tool for those underground bands who found themselves cast aside by the mainstream media.

Merseyside band Rosetta Stone made great use of this 'new-fangled' tool. Plucked out by The Mission's Wayne Hussey, they were one of the new UK goth acts who were tipped for great things but never quite made the headlining grade through a combination of bad luck and modest media attention. For them, the internet became an essential means of promoting their music and frontman Porl King frequently popped up on the newly-created text-only newsgroup uk.people.gothic, which became a thriving UK network with a large amount of traffic. Former promoter and webzine editor Michael Johnson adds: "In the '90s, the internet made goth work. It gave goth an essential tool – an all-purpose communications nexus. It was the key element in the rise of the 'underground' goth scene of the '90s. Nothing else – not the Marquee goth nights in London, not the Whitby Gothic Weekend, no other elements of the '90s scene, no matter how good in themselves – could have pulled goth up without that vital link between everything."

The absence of any media network supporting and publicising UK goth

Rosetta Stone in West Hampstead circa 1995 © Mick Mercer

Stephan Groth from Apoptygma Berzerk. © Tarjei Ekenes Krogh

France's fluorescent cyberpunks Punish Yourself © Punish Yourself

during this time and the limitations of the internet in the early days meant the scene was undergoing metamorphosis in some areas and remaining constant in others. What had continued from the 1980s now became referred to as "trad goth" while a new dark electronic dance movement that had come over from Europe earned itself the tag of "cybergoth" and went day-glo.

The German wave scene had long been associated with electronic music as had the early UK and Canadian post-punk scenes but a new breed of European bands were about to really turn things up a notch. In Norway, a style of music was being developed that was based around synth-pop, industrial and EBM but it retained the darkness of goth – Norway's independent label Tatra Productions, Belgium's Alfa Matrix (run alongside *Side Line Magazine*) and Germany's Dependent became strongly associated with it. Bands like Apoptygma Berzerk and Icon Of Coil came from this scene and worked in harmony with what Sweden's Covenant and Belgium's Suicide Commando were doing. In time, this electronic style would become harder and harsher with influences from other countries like Mexico (Hocico) and Germany's own :wumpscut:.

In Belgium, where Front 242 had been perfecting EBM for some time, and nearby in France, electronic music was increasing in popularity as well. Self-proclaimed 'Batcave' band Punish Yourself ended up following the trend rather unwittingly when they lost their drummer and used drum machines rather than find a physical replacement. "We realised we were listening a lot to bands like Ministry, Skinny Puppy and Front 242," frontman Vx remembers, "so we decided to try to play this music we liked to dance to [but] we never put our Batcave roots aside and the French goth audience was always our audience of choice. We had always been fans of more visual bands like Alien Sex Fiend so we wore heavy make-up, which we discovered almost by accident looked amazing under UV lights." The band now refer to themselves as fluorescent cyberpunks and perform wearing UV-reactive body paint.

In the UK, cybergoth took its inspiration from Japanese anime, cyberpunk and mainstream dance clubs. It was especially popular on the Scottish goth scene where it would frequently be crossed over with hard house and in Nottingham, the club Cyberpolis would go on to issue their own compilation CD. But cybergoth was alternately embraced and shunned by the gothic movement for bringing new blood to the scene at the expensive of more traditional gothic rock sounds. Ronan Harris from Irish electro group VNV Nation coined the term 'future-pop' to describe his band's music and it certainly seemed that cyber was welcome far more in popular culture than goth ever had been – even Take That's Robbie Williams was snapped in the audience for Bristol-based band Mesh! If goth had originally been about being serious and melancholic then cybergoth was the complete opposite. It was about having fun, wearing crazy vibrant clothing and had very little to do with

politics or trying to get a message across, although some bands such as VNV Nation preferred their music to have meaning. Some even argued that it wasn't a relevant part of the goth scene because it had nothing to do with its original aims and perhaps that was true but what it did do was revive an interest in the movement and quash many bad stereotypes that had arisen through the press during the decline of gothic rock in the mainstream. "I've always found the great guitar/bleep schism which divides goth into two opposing camps rather artificial," says Michael Johnson. He adds: "Nobody who grew up listening to the John Peel show could ring-fence their musical taste like that." Opposing camps or not, one thing that the cybergoth explosion did was apparently increase the popularity of clubbing at the expense of live gigs – a development that had already impacted the mainstream music scene.

Parts of the pure goth scene tried to merge more deliberately with cybergoth; the Darkbeat label was founded to cover some of the new types of British electro-goth music that was starting to be made. Set up by Glenn Wilson, one part of the band Faithful Dawn, its roster included Bristol-based bands Nekromantik, Sneaky Bat Machine and The Narcissus Pool who all existed on a small but healthy scale with scene gigs and appearances at the Whitby Gothic Weekend.

But perhaps the media didn't realise that this rave-friendly subgenre was part of the new goth scene because whenever it attempted another pot-shot, it would focus on what was now a rather out-dated idea of the subculture. During the 1990s, followers of vampire literature and movies would often get mislabelled as goths and end up on television or in magazines, bearing plastic fangs, capes and coffins, which caused a backlash in some parts of the scene who felt this was all rather passé and a bit sad. Separate vampire appreciation societies like Thee Vampire Guild, Whitby Dracula Society and The London Vampire Group sprung up and were occasionally invited over goth's threshold to take the edge off all the fuss and eventually it did dampen down only to be replaced by a retaliation against goth being lumped in with the metal scene a few years later!

Similarly goth was mistaken for part of the fetish scene during this time as well although admittedly it had been borrowing a few wardrobe staples from there for quite a while! There was a degree of crossover – The Batcave had, afterall, attracted a similarly deviant crowd – but the downside was an influx of amateur photographers trying to take inappropriate photos of gothic girls and increased verbal hassle on the streets. It probably didn't help that an alternative porn movement had started to emerge in LA partly through numerous photographers, various websites and adult movies. Live action role-

Vampiric goths BloodLust and Katie Korpse at the Whitby
Gothic Weekend circa 1999 © Stephen Milward

playing of a non-sexual nature (LARP) had also started cropping up as brought in by some of the geeks and gamers who'd become drawn to the scene (often realising long hair and black clothing made them more popular with members of the opposite sex!). This benign and small-scale involvement would later tarnish festivals like Whitby Gothic Weekend and Wave Gotik Treffen, which would attract large numbers of 'normals' in fancy dress, who apparently misunderstood goth's relevance as a musical subculture as well as a fashion-based one.

But for all this, the UK goth scene stuck two fingers up at the negative press it had received when Scottish fanzine *Naked Truth* printed up a run of black t-shirts with the words "Sad Old Goth" emblazoned in huge white letters on the front. This self-depreciatingly humorous design went on to become the best-selling tee in Nightbreed's mail order catalogue.

THE DARK SCENE

If the UK scene was in a bit of a muddle with all these different genres, the German scene had the perfect solution. By the mid-1990s, the phrase Schwarze Szene (literally translated as the Black, or Dark Scene) started to become popular as a large umbrella under which all these dark musical styles – including many others – could be placed. Such a term has not only boosted the commercial appeal of this scene but it also opened up the gates to a number of smaller scenes, which might not otherwise have had a look-in.

"There was a massive network of youth clubs in Germany," remembers Nightbreed's Trevor Bamford, "and you could literally just tour that circuit. Over there, the alternative magazines and record labels had funding from the government too, so all that helped support the scene whereas in the UK, we never had any of that." Once a mere follower of trends, Germany was beginning to set them and with a thriving underground support network, this grandiose umbrella was opened up as wide as possible to capture many different styles from the straight-forward post-punk and gothic rock through to the more specialist post-apocalyptic folk, EBM (electronic body music, as coined by the Belgium electronic project Front 242) and 'mittelalter' styles of music.

But not everything is as rosy as it might sound: "The German media hate gothic!" says Catastrophe Ballet frontman Eric Burton, who is also general manager of the music promotions company Hard Beat. "If you're from the scene and say you're a gothic, they laugh at you and think you sleep in a coffin or stupid shit like that but they don't really distinguish between true gothic and the Schwarze Szene. To them, anything that has a moody element or is clothed in black is gothic!" In fact, to many of the younger generation,

A staged medieval 'battle' in the Wave Gotik Treffen's Heidnisches Dorf or Pagan Village.
© Stephen Milward

The distinctive Mittelalter look
© Stephen Milward

At Leipzig's Wave Gotik Treffen, now the largest dark gathering in the world.
© Stephen Milward

Mittelalter band In Extremo © Universal Music

the Schwarze Szene is the German goth scene but for the older generation, goth is just one part of its many facets.

Ralf Epke came into the scene in the mid-1990s, inspired by the songs of German electro-darkwave act Silke Bischoff, who are now known as 18 Summers. "I lost three people who were close to me," he explains. "People assumed I was gothic because I was wearing dark clothing so I started to explore what this meant and found these sad songs matched my mood and helped with my grieving." As he got more interested, his gothic education followed the electronic path via a CD from the Swedish Star-Trek-obsessed synth-poppers S.P.O.C.K. Now a fan of electronic genres like EBM and aggrotech, he runs the German gothic clothing label Re-Agenz and is a self-proclaimed gothic.

But not everything that German goths embrace is blacker than black. Mittelalter is a rather complex genre that is now welcomed as part of the ever-expanding Schwarze Szene even though it originally had absolutely nothing to do with goth and many of the older goths maintain it still doesn't. It translates literally as 'medieval' and encompasses anything from straight-forward old-fashioned Latin hymns through to the more modern hybrid of medieval metal. Its more contemporary roots lay in some of the experimental elements of Dead Can Dance's music and Italy's Ataraxia, which inspired the beautiful melodies that Austrian band Qntal make (founded by Deine Lakaien's Ernst Horn).

Mittelalter as a musical genre is generally agreed to have come about with the formation of Corvus Corax in 1989. Using traditional instruments and original Latin manuscripts, the East German collective soon found themselves being referred to as a "bagpipe band" for their unusual but very infectious sound. Scoring their early gigs through Germany's network of medieval markets and fairs, these bands started filtering through into the Schwarze Szene and then into goth via the medium of dance. It was the harder, more metal-orientated bands like Subway To Sally and In Extremo that helped move this eclectic blend of music out of the re-enactment fares and into the clubs. In 1996, Corvus Corax frontman Teufel started a new trend by founding the mittelalter-meets-industrial-metal side project Tanzwut, which acted as a direct bridge across what should be several opposing genres. Saltatio Mortis, Schemeish and Letz Instanz join them now as the genre's big bands and just as goth has its own look, so does mittelalter. It's a big old excuse to dress up in traditional medieval outfits with the infamous Snakebite and Black replaced by various different types of mead drunk straight from a cleaned animal horn. Just as the original Gothic tribe came from Scandinavia and settled in parts of Germany, this is acknowledged through the use of Norse anachronisms like the Viking horns, small bells traditionally used to ward off evil and jewellery in the shape of Thor's hammer. Celtic influence is also prevalent in the guise of long kilts, more symbolic jewellery and the very popular bagpipes that give this kind of music its distinctive sound.

The cross-pollenisation of medieval with industrial and metal most probably couldn't have come about were it not for another German sub-scene that kicked off around 1995. A new electronic band called Rammstein had just released their debut album *Herzeleid* and, in an attempt to place it somewhere appropriate, the term Neue Deutsche Härte (new German hardness) was coined by the media. Normally lumped in with the industrial-metal genre, NDH managed to cross over into the German goth, hard rock and industrial dance scenes, bringing fans from each genre to the big Schwarze party and further increasing numbers. This would be an important development that would not only boost the commercial viability of the German goth scene but also form a greater rift with the UK scene, which was still very much stuck in an '80s rut despite attempts from gothic metal bands like Creaming Jesus and 13 Candles to liven things up a bit.

As the Schwarze Szene expanded in Germany, so it was supported by clubs, gigs and festivals. In particular, the Wave Gotik Treffen grew in size and venues over the course of several years, to become what is now the world's largest gothic festival. Although its change has been very gradual, it has played an important role in the development of the country's gothic subculture as followers have used it as a guide for contemporary music and fashion. Ronny Moorings remembers his band Clan Of Xymox's first visit to the city for the WGT in 1997: "I thought Leipzig looked very depressing and pitied the people having to live there. So much has changed there since then – people would not recognise it anymore. It looks almost like it used to in its heyday; a monumental city that's green, beautiful and quite unique." Moorings has since relocated there.

All this seemed quite a contrast to what was going on in the UK. British band Every New Dead Ghost toured there – its lead singer Trevor Bamford, now in Midnight Configuration, remembers discovering a whole new world: "There were these metal mags like *Zillo* that had these big gothic sections in, covering what they called 'The Ghostriders Of German Gothic'. There were these great new bands like Das Ich, Project Pitchfork and Sweet William all coming out of the scene… The German music mags never demonised it like the *NME* and *Melody Maker*, they valued all art for what it was and a whole support network grew out of that. [In the UK] the mainstream media pretended goth didn't exist anymore but there was still a scene and it was hungry for more."

Bamford and Suspiria's Mark Tansley set up a label and mail order catalogue called Nightbreed Recordings to sell these new bands he'd discovered in Germany. Nightbreed expanded to a label and small shop just outside Nottingham. Resurrection Music and Grave News Ltd were founded in

London to serve a similar purpose and all three companies worked alongside each other importing and exporting new gothic sounds. Several years later, the more electronic-orientated Cryonica Recordings came along and the role of all these labels was to be absolutely crucial in keeping the UK's underground goth scene alive and kicking.

THE NEW DARK WAVE?

By the late 1990s, the goth scene had become synthesised and assimilated by so many other styles, it was a different creature from its early post-punk years; it would go on to change even more in the new millennium. Where the original key players of the scene had once been the UK and the US for deathrock, Germany and Scandinavia were now holding more musical and stylistic influence. Although the purists argue even to this day the relevance of gothic metal to the gothic subculture, the style has since become merged with the even more bombastic symphonic metal. This has subsequently given birth

Simone Simons gives an explosive performance with Epica at Female Metal Voices in 2008
© Stephen Milward

Gothic and symphonic metal have influenced contemporary gothic fashion
© Stephen Milward

to dramatic female-fronted bands like Tarja-era Nightwish, Epica and Within Temptation whose powerful vocalists wear theatrical gowns on stage as if they were performing in an opera rather than a rock concert. Likewise their stage shows frequently contain pyrotechnics and scenery for a full-on performance which forms quite a contrast to the dry ice and colour lights of bands like The Sisters Of Mercy. Interestingly in the Netherlands, Within Temptation have always been regarded as a part of the underground goth scene even though their sound has more recently become closer meshed with European metal. Yet their dramatic look filtered down through the different layers of the goth scene, working harmoniously with the trend towards extravagant costumes. "The Germans just seemed to get it and listened without prejudice," Greg Mackintosh from Paradise Lost remembers. "We had to become popular in mainland Europe before the UK would entertain us... and for some reason the Finnish took to this with particular aplomb. It was like they had been waiting all their lives for this style of music."

Embraced by Germany's Schwarze Szene and the darker Scandinavian music movements, these bands certainly have gothic elements to their sound and image but they have little to do with the early post-punk roots of goth. DJ and gig promoter Martin Oldgoth is one of those who fell into the goth scene through punk's back door and sums up this time of change: "[In the 1990s] we saw the inclusion of so many of what I thought were unwelcome genres: metal, industrial, EBM, all of which watered it down and none of which in my opinion have any real place in a scene born from the ashes of punk ... I hate the term 'trad' goth; it's as if goth in itself no longer has a meaning unless it has prefix to define which 'type' it is. In my mind, goth is goth and the rest just isn't."

His opinion is shared by a number of goth traditionalists but as Norwegian musician Mortiis argues: "You know if you're interested in music, does it matter? Is crossing musical styles going to *ruin* your scene, I mean ... really? Are you kidding me, how can that happen? That sounds very elitist to me. I guess at the end of the day you can split people like that in two categories: the people into it for the show, and the people that are into it for the music it produces. I'm into the music ... I have a hard time taking the other group seriously ... I love the show, and we do that shit too, but at the end of the day, it started with the music for me and that's where it'll end."

Even in Finland, where goth in the 1980s and early '90s shared the stage with electronic music – Advanced Art, Chaingun Operate and Shade Factory were among those who often played with the darker acts – it's been rock and metal that have successfully crossed over with the darkside. HIM's 'love metal' and former glam band The 69 Eyes' blend of goth 'n' roll (a term they borrowed from Sweden's Funhouse) saw them marketed as gothic poster boys for a new generation although parts of the underground scene argued they were simply cashing in on the movement. DJ Santtu remembers: "When the metal scene started going mainstream, [those] bands brought about a new interest in goth. It's interesting but those who were most accountable for the rise of the scene seldom got the credit for it [and] it seemed the more attention a band got abroad, the more they were mocked by the scene itself." It was almost parallel to what was happening in the UK with the gothic metal genre, which had apparently been disowned by the more traditional goths themselves even though it was bringing new interest to the scene.

The 69 Eyes frontman Jyrki remembers: "We were inspired by bands like The Cult and Lords Of The New Church as well as the '90s dark American rock like Type O Negative [and] had been dressed in black, singing about horror movies and vampires ever since we started [in 1989]. We were experimenting with modern sounds when all of sudden HIM started a new scene in Finland which was considered to be gothic metal…and naturally we got our share of local and international attention as well. It felt a bit uncomfortable since we were not metal and had already been playing and recording for about ten years. But on the other hand HIM opened up doors [as they were] the most popular band in central Europe and Finland back then."

Over in Russia, Agatha Christie were continuing to enjoy a healthy underground career although their sound gradually shifted to reflect the popularity for more synth-driven music. The scene there has subsequently given birth to Phantom Bertha and more recently the trio Otto Dix among a score of other bands whose names are only readable to those proficient in Russian! Although few of the popular goth bands have played there, the proximity of the sea and more political freedom means ample opportunities for Russian goths to take a boat trip over to the wealthier Helsinki. Not only are there more chances for clothing and music shopping but also the city's adequately-sized venues like Tavastia, Nosturi and Gloria have hosted many dark music concerts over the years. Just as the goth scene was originally just part of the alternative scene in the UK, in many parts of the world it still forms just a small part of an otherwise larger genre.

By the end of the '90s, things had dramatically changed in the former Eastern Bloc, where a small but active scene continued to thrive. Estonia and the Ukraine are now catered for by the *Ukrainian Gothic Portal* – a printed magazine and promotions agency that began working for the gothic and electro scenes in the former Soviet Republic around 1999. The new wave of Eastern European goth has helped bring about new artists like Estonia's electro-industrial noise merchant Evestus (previously part of metal band Solwaig), Ukraine's experimental Crazy Juliette who refer to their style as 'fairy wave', the Russian-Ukrainian darkwave of The Nightchild and Croatia's Sisters-inspired Phantasmagoria who supported The Mission in Zagreb back in 2008 and shouldn't be confused with the Japanese band of the same name.

Towards the end of the 1990s and early 2000s, healthy deathrock and horror punk scenes started to grow in Slovakia and Poland with bands like The Last Days Of Jesus and Miguel And The Living Dead emerging. Their tongue-in-cheek fast-paced music offered an alternative to the more political punk and rockabilly movements that had been born from years of civil unrest in the Eastern Bloc – Slovakia even established its very own regular Batcave night in 1996.

The Czech Republic, Slovakia and Poland's goth scenes now seem to be more greatly influenced by German trends when it comes to music and fashion, which are all a lot more elaborate than might be expected. The Czech Republic has been hosting its very own Prague Gothic Treffen, Bratislava in Slovakia has become a hot spot for touring bands like Paradise Lost and Skinny Puppy and the independent Castle Party festival has been attracting impressive line-ups in Poland since the mid-1990s. Held in the appropriately gothic setting of Bolków Castle, its geographic location means it's easy to get to and tends to attract a very vibrant crowd of goths from all over.

At the beginning of the millennium, a group of fans got together to form CZ Sanctuary, which acts as both a promotions agency and website for goth in the Czech Republic. They're also responsible for the Prague Gothic Treffen, which is held annually and attracts several hundred goths although these days there seems to be more interest in the electronic music side of things there than with gothic rock. Recently-reformed EBM act Vanessa and the electro-industrial Depressive Disorder are among the popular local bands.

But not everywhere has embraced goth – Denmark and the Netherlands in particular had always been rather slow to pick up on the music. There,

Evestus from Estonia
© Evestus

electronic and metal bands are more popular although the Dutch gothic rock band Malochia tried to push through the cobwebs in the mid-1990s but, like Clan Of Xymox, found more success in Germany. Dutch goth Marloes muses: "When the synthesisers improved and dance music got really popular by the late '80s, the Netherlands saw [more potential in this style, which] lead to Eurodance and house acts. The goth scene ... saw more future here and was able to develop in the electronic scene while the guitar-side miserably died out in the late '80s. It was a question about which musical-sound offered more future, and clearly electronic music won."

LAND OF THE RISING SUN

While a new wave of goth was keeping Germany busy, something similar was happening in the Far East. Japan had dipped a toe into the murky waters of goth back in the early '80s with post-punk like Auto-Mod and Phaidia. Clearly inspired by American deathrock, their sounds were characterised by fast-paced riff-centred gothic punk with wardrobes being toned down versions of post-punk that were quite at odds with the saccharine-sweet sounds of the commercial J-pop and electronic disco music that were around at the time. On the live circuit, their harsh-edged music contrasted with Western goth bands like The Cure and Siouxsie And The Banshees who were welcomed by local audiences in the early part of the 1980s. Influenced by larger-than-life street fashion, a new subcultural movement slowly started to evolve in Japan.

But by the late '90s a fashion-oriented genre of rock music called visual kei would revive interest in the gothic subculture in Japan even though its only real relevance to goth was that it too had been inspired by punk. The term 'visual kei' was coined by Yoshiki Hayashi, the drummer from Tokyo metal band X (later called X Japan to distinguish themselves from an American act with the same name). Realising the importance of a strong image, the band developed a unique look with huge hair and unusual outfits and went on to become the county's answer to Kiss. Around the same time in Osaka, a visually vibrant glam band called Color was also gaining popularity – they too came to adopt the visual kei moniker and the two bands represented the East and West of this new musical and fashion movement. Hiroshi Tomioka, aka Dynamite Tommy, from Color explains his inspiration: "In ancient Japan, people lived honoring their values and eccentric-looking people were called Kabuki Artists, so I wanted to look original [and] eccentric."

As X Japan and Color's fanbases grew, so did their style with Hayashi feminising his look by wearing more traditional kimonos which made him stand out. It didn't take long before the fashion shops started to recreate the band's stagewear for young fans who would spend thousands of yen on looking like their idols, a practice referred to in Japanese culture as 'cosplay'. By the mid-1990s, visual kei had become a mainstream trend with Jpop and Jrock bands fashioning themselves in similar attire. But it wasn't just about emulating heroes. In Tokyo's trendy Harajuku district, young fashionistas were developing their own street styles, publicised by picture-heavy magazines like *Fruits* and through this a style called lolita became extremely fashionable.

Elegant Gothic Lolitas in Tokyo.
© Stephen Milward

PSYDOLL

Japan's Psydoll © Psydoll

Although cute lolita fashions had been around since the late '70s, the popularity of these new feminine-looking visual kei bands increased its appeal and, as visual kei moved away from its glam roots towards a darker, heavier sound, so lolita dress moved away from white and pink frills to something a lot edgier. Two bands stand out as being responsible: Dir En Grey and Malice Mizer.

Formed in 1997 from rock band La:Sadie's, Dir En Grey's early career saw them closely affiliated with X Japan as Hayashi produced their early singles and their image bordered on cosplay. Within a few years though, they had started to move away from that and find their own sound, which was a progressive blend of Japanese rock and Western industrial metal, complemented by a look that mixed their visual kei roots with S&M gothic wear. Leather, bondage restraints and jewel coloured hair extensions gave them a much darker feel. Founding guitarist Kaoru explains: "We just wanted to be different, to create an illusion that we weren't people on stage but some other thing. Everything that we saw was an inspiration; same with our music." And of their choice of gothic clothing, he adds: "It was because we ourselves were very dark people. We're more attracted to things which are negative."

The band signed to Free-Will, the label owned by Dyamite Tommy who remembers: "In the early '00s many Dir En Grey fans thought the band looked goth, I think that brought an influence to how people viewed the band too. The Dir En Grey you see today look nothing like they did back then but their resolve has not changed … it's still as strong and amazing as before."

Just as Dir En Grey played with the whole gothic rock image, there was another band that really went to town with the more romantic look. Malice Mizer formed in 1992 with keyboard player/guitarists Mana and Közi – Mana was originally in the punk band Girl'e before joining Matenrou, where he met Közi. Whereas the earlier visual kei bands had mostly derived their influences from metal, Malice Mizer borrowed elements of goth as well as classical music and progressive metal while their look was even more unique. Taking inspiration from French Romanticism and later Victoriana, Mana is credited with creating the gothic lolita look, which literally crossed lolita with the more traditional Victorian gothic look that was gaining popularity in the West at the time. In rare interviews, Mana has claimed that he combined the two simply because he liked them both and he quickly became the member seen by many as responsible for creating the band's image. Black lace replaced lolita's pink frills and crucifix-patterned brocade was used instead of cute prints with heavier make-up to enhance the look – Mana founded his own clothing company in 1999 called Moi-même-Moitié so fans could buy his designs, which are often referred to as Elegant Gothic Lolita and the more masculine style of the Elegant Gothic Aristocrat. Musically Malice Mizer sound nothing like the early post-punk bands that goth was born from nor do they sound like the second generation of gothic rock, made popular by the likes of The Sisters Of Mercy and Fields Of The Nephilim, so by that merit they're difficult to place in the gothic genre other than just as a visual inspiration and the occasional bit of influence from horror movies. Naturally the underground Japanese goth scene has always dismissed them as a metal band yet Mana's gothic leanings contributed greatly not only to gothic fashion in Japan, which even has its own department stores, but also to the West's gothic subculture. The weighty periodical *Gothic And Lolita Bible* joined visual kei mags like *Shoxx, Cure* and its more mainstream parent publication *Kera* as a popular fashion and lifestyle purchase for Japanese teens. The hard-backed publication featured not just articles on fashion and Japanese bands but also covered acts that fell under the Western goth banner like The Cure and Bauhaus. All this strengthened the country's actual, and still very underground, goth scene. However, visual kei remained predominantly a young movement as Japanese society is predominantly conformist and far less likely to dress extravagantly than European music fans. It's interesting to see that the Gothic Lolita look has now been adopted by older women, as well as some men, since it has been exported from Japan.

Malice Mizer went on indefinite hiatus in 2001 after the death of drummer Kami; Mana founded the record label Midi:Nette and set about work on a new project called Moi-Dix-Mois. Electronic duo Schwarz Stein were signed to Midi:Nette, while gothic-industrial band Psydoll, Candy Spooky Theatre and the harsher Gothika who have located to Germany are among those who've since enjoyed moderate success outside the country. But within a few years, the visual kei scene started to show some signs of crossing outside Japan. One band that helped this was Syaranosui. They were unique in that they not only featured two women but one of them was British – visual kei bands had traditionally been a bit of a men's club with female fans viewing any woman as direct competition. Former gothic model Rosi Aconite co-founded the band under the stage name of Rosalie although she left two years later and was replaced by an all-Japanese line-up. However her involvement and well-blogged fascination with contemporary Japanese music and fashion helped raise interest in the genre outside the East even though visual kei was frequently misinterpreted as goth because of its strong image. Transplanted UK gothic-electro band Sins Of The Flesh and BLOOD, from Osaka, would continue that interest which assimilated with Western goth culture. Starting off as more of a visual kei metal band, BLOOD's sound has gradually developed into something not unlike the electronic darkwave of LA band London After Midnight. "The word 'gothic' has only really been used for the last ten years or so but it's really not a very big scene," says founding member Kiwamu. His label Darkest Labyrinth and Deathwatch Asia, owned by Sins Of The Flesh's Jamie Nova, are two of Japan's only Jgoth record companies, aiming to point those interested in the darker end of visual kei in the right direction. Kiwamu explains: "I think a lot of people here don't know the difference between visual kei and gothic. I think fans started to get confused when the visual kei bands started using black costumes and make-up and just assumed they were gothic too. Many Japanese bands mix different styles together, whether it's gothic, glam, metal or new wave, so Japanese bands make their own style and that's what visual kei is really about – it's making your own style from lots of different things."

Elsewhere in Singapore, a dark alternative scene has been growing since the '90s, supported by online communities called Singapore Goth Covenant and Singapore Dark Alternative Movement. Gothic gigs, clubs and clothing shops run on a small scale and there are a handful of underground bands like Cervix Couch (who take their name from a Christian Death song), the industrial Dualtone and gothic metal act Meza Virs. There the scene is less about visual kei and more about imported goth music, with electronic genres and the cyber look being particularly popular. Singapore's geographic position means its musical influence is derived as much from Australia as from Japan and this has really helped diversify the scene. Gothic entrepreneur Saito Nagasaki, who left the country briefly to study in Australia, puts himself at the centre of Singapore's gothic movement as he has been responsible in helping to build its local club scene and raising its profile in the media.

Nearby the goth scenes in Thailand and the Philippines operate on a similar hybrid, but with greater emphasis on gothic metal. This is all reflected in the gothic power metal of local bands like the female-fronted Cherub, the doomy Breathless and the very popular symphonic Dear Sinner, although the gothic clubs there tend to favour electronic sounds from the West or Jrock.

THE NEW WORLD ORDER

If a quasi-gothic subculture was taking Japan by storm then something similar was starting to happen in the US. Deathrock pioneers Christian Death, now fronted by Valor Kand, were gradually following a more metal path and Rozz Williams' suicide in 1998 finally scuppered any last hopes of the original line-up reuniting. But his influence wasn't lost on a work experience journalism student from Florida called Brian Warner who had managed to blag an interview with hot new electro-industrial act Nine Inch Nails. Warner was part of an underground metal band called Marilyn Manson And The Spooky Kids and took his stage name from a hybrid of two of America's biggest celebrity dichotomies: Marilyn Monroe and Charles Manson. After a brief foray working with alternative rock band Jack Off Jill, he turned his attentions towards his band's own debut *Portrait Of An American Family* which was

produced by The Swans' Roli Mosimann. Riddled with drug references, the somewhat insipid metal album gained him some recognition in the underground scene but it wasn't until NIN's Trent Reznor acted as executive producer on its conceptual studio follow-up *The Antichrist Superstar* that he really started getting noticed. Along with assistance from Skinny Puppy mastermind Dave 'Rave' Ogilvie and Sean Beavan who'd also mixed *Pretty Hate Machine*, a contemporary industrial-metal album was crafted that that would see Manson later lumped into the same category as Ministry and Fear Factory. From the tribal, deathrock drumming on 'Beautiful People' to the hauntingly sinister ballad 'Man That You Fear', the album rapidly became a commercial success in the US and started to spread out to Europe.

Manson's look, with his long black hair and corpse-like make-up, was influenced by Rozz Williams' early image and he would go on to name-check him as an inspiration in interviews. "I wonder if Marilyn Manson and Nine Inch Nails would so easily have delved into the darker realms without deathrock and goth," muses Christian Death's former keyboardist Gitane Demone. "They found a way to commercialise it – maybe the timing was just right."

Frequently performing in surgical garments splashed with blood, which initially appeared to be his own, Manson took the schlock rock of Kiss and Alice Cooper to a more literal level. His black clothing – often designer garments – bruised eyes and tattoos became a popular look for youngsters who would refer to themselves as goths. While many dismissed Marilyn Manson as being little more than a commercial metal band, their dark music and horror-inspired look became gradually assimilated into contemporary goth culture, which adapted accordingly. Trevor Bamford from Midnight Configuration and UK label Nightbreed says cautiously: "I get called a heretic for defending the gothic metal movement but if you don't embrace new ideas then a scene becomes inbred."

America's new gothic metal movement opened the doors for other bands to follow. Brooklyn doom

Kate's Clothing remodels the black trench coat, which became a wardrobe essential thanks to *The Crow* and *The Matrix*.

metallers Type O Negative incorporated softer elements into their music and even parodied the look in the song 'Black No. 1', while Rob Zombie broke away from his metal band White Zombie and pursued a successful career mixing horror with industrial-metal.

The popularity of the 1994 graphic novel-turned movie *The Crow* further raised goth's profile with its dark soundtrack featuring songs by The Cure, The Jesus And Mary Chain and Nine Inch Nails covering Joy Division's 'Dead Souls'. Starring Brandon Lee, the movie tells the story of musician Eric Draven who is murdered on his wedding night and brought back to life to avenge his and his fiancee's death by supernatural forces that take the form of a crow. Not only did the story and music resonate but the protagonist's wardrobe inspired – it consisted of black leather and trench coats, which were adopted by goths not only Stateside but also across the rest of the world. US chain store Hot Topic were quick to pick up on the trend with a range of easy-to-wear, off-the-peg gothic clothing based around the more expensive designs that exclusive alternative manufacturers sold. Black lipstick and nail polish, once the reserve of Halloween fancy dress or theatrical supplies, became easy to find and punk brand Manic Panic found their unusual shades of hair dye copied and mass produced by retailers jumping on the bandwagon. It's here the phrase "Hot Topic Goth" comes from and it became used to describe anyone whose style came straight out of a mall style book without any customisation or creativity. But for every commercial scene there is always an underbelly and as gothic metal and gothic industrial were becoming popular in the mainstream, the gothic underground was busy revolting against it!

Underground clothing manufacturers sprung up all over the place thanks to the popularity of the internet and America's geography made this new method of communication extremely popular. Just as the UK had its own uk.people.gothic newsgroup, alt.gothic was preferred by those in the US and a gothic festival called Convergence was formed by some of its members. A record label called Projekt was founded by Sam Rosenthal from the gothic shoegaze band Black Tape For A Blue Girl. It specialised in more ethereal sounds that were quite the antithesis of the noisy racket the mainstream was calling goth and this more gentle side was being reflected in fashion which focused more on floaty, hippyish styles that worked in parallel with the UK's pagan/goth scene compared to the PVC and ripped fishnets that were still being worked in LA's more fetishy gothic metal movement.

In between what the US mainstream thought was gothic and the real underground, the electronic scene was also enjoying an increase in popularity among this dark alternative subculture just as it was out in Europe. Newer rockier bands such as Chemlab and 16Volt appeared alongside '80s industrial acts like Skinny Puppy and KMFDM and the term 'rivethead' started to crop up as a description of a military-inspired look that industrial fans adopted.

Chemlab also used the term on the title of a song from their 1993 debut album *Burn Out At The Hydrogen Bar* and that look would quickly start filtering across into other countries.

Out in the Netherlands, Clan Of Xymox's Ronny Moorings noticed a definite shift towards more electronic music as well: "It had started at the end of the '80s, maybe early '90s with musicians looking ahead and trying out different styles, including me. It was a result of house music creeping from the underground into the daylight, inspiring musicians to take another route. It was almost as exiting as the punk movement twenty years before."

Something similar was also happening in Greece and South Africa where it was beginning to engulf what was already a compact goth scene there. The industrial-metal sounds of Marilyn Manson, Nine Inch Nails and Rammstein that were played in goth nights around major cities like Johannesburg, Cape Town and Durban provided fans with a gateway to the real gothic scene, which was surviving through a combination of DIY ethics and imported goods. Political and racial tensions had settled down somewhat by the late '90s when the South African scene started to emulate the UK's cybergoth movement. Gothic rock was pushed further into the undergrowth as Raymond Ross from Ankst recalls: "Dave [Ankst's keyboardist] and I found ourselves being approached constantly by the old school and traditional goths, asking us please to reconsider starting something up again, but we constantly declined. That was until at one of these events that it struck me like a sledge hammer as I sat at my table watching luminously clad 'ravers' grooving to the pulsing beat of a re-remix of a remix of some obscure bedroom produced EBM track, I had to ask myself: *Is this what our precious scene has been reduced to?*"

Bands like Celtic Rumours, who sounded like a cross between The Bolshoi and The Mission, and Penguins In Bondage with their reverb and 4/4 beats were making enough music to keep this alternative dark scene happy. But there was one South African goth band who managed to surpass anyone's expectations and that was Johannesburg's The Awakening. Formed in 1995 by singer/guitarist Ashton Nyte, the band went on to become the very first gothic act to not only headline the country's major music festivals but to sign a deal with a European label. Their seventh studio album *Razor Burn* was released through Germany's Massacre Records and raised their profile outside their home country. They relocated to the US a year after its 2006 release – the band continues to tour there and Nyte is working on developing his solo career. Durban's Ankst, who formed in 2006, now flag themselves up as South Africa's only goth band.

Over in Canada in the '90s, things were also taking a decidedly electric path, influenced by the sounds of '80s post-punk/industrial bands like Skinny Puppy. But just as the goth scene of the '90s had moved away from rock music and towards electronic, it would shift again. The first indications of its new direction came from Quebec's French-speaking city Montreal, where the goth scene had sprung from the new wave and alternative music movements and so the path was cleared for a different musical style. Although local goth bands were few and far between in the city, Santeria and Bordello were among those to emerge in the '90s, albeit with a more rockabilly feel to their sound, going back to the early days of the post-punk scene with the likes of The Cramps and Stray Cats. "We started off more of a dark glam rock type band originally," explains Coffin Joe, formerly of Bordello. "But over the years with a few changes in band members, we took on more of a deathrock twist. Unfortunately not many really twisted our way here, so after more line-up changes, we went for a more accessible but still dark sound and have now changed our name to The Crypt Club."

Joe now works at Montreal's gothic shop Cruella and, while the scene there is still very heavily influenced by EBM and industrial, there has been a noticeable image shift. "Back when we started [in 1996], I remember velvet was definitely the way to go. Every girl wanted a velvet skirt or dress and guys wanted either pirate shirts or skin-tight fishnet tops. Now we've had a big boost from horror movie culture, which has mostly been driven by our psychobilly scene," he explains.

MIDDLE EASTERN PROMISE

If the 1990s were goth's true peak, then it shouldn't come as too much of a surprise that it managed to spread its wings and travel to some very far-flung

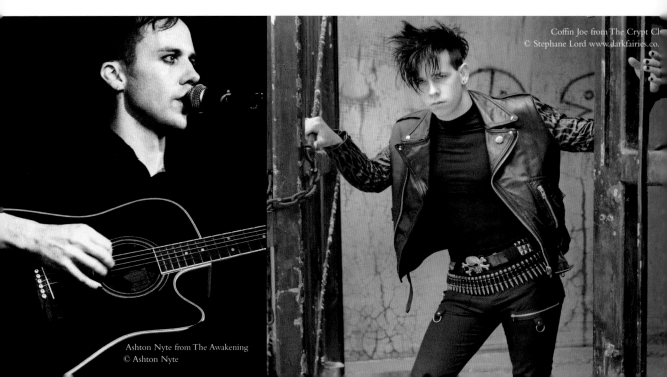

Coffin Joe from The Crypt Cl[...]
© Stephane Lord www.darkfairies.co.[...]

Ashton Nyte from The Awakening
© Ashton Nyte

destinations in that time. Back in the early days, the goth scene took its influences from many different sources. From literature and movies to other musical scenes like glam and rockabilly, there are few areas it hasn't tapped into – even country and western wasn't safe! Yet one of the most endearing influences has to be the Middle East. Siouxsie Sioux might have sung about 'Arabian Knights' and draped herself in traditional costume for the video but the alternative music scene in Arabian countries is rather more complex than in other areas.

Alternative subcultures don't sit well within Sharia law but that doesn't mean they don't exist. In these areas, goth tends to be lumped in with metal and be seen more as just a darker type of music rather than a separate subculture. It goes without saying that the internet has played a huge role in helping spread Western music styles to these strict societies. Rock music presenter Somi Arian was born and brought up in a poor area in the south of Tehran where she stumbled across forbidden music purely by accident: "In the Middle East in general the entire metal scene is under surveillance and frowned upon. Iran especially is an Islamic country and music in general is very restricted, especially rock and metal," she explains. "The government in Iran associates metal music and [the] gothic style of dressing and make-up with devil worshipping – people can get arrested for openly revealing their leaning towards such a lifestyle." The documentary *Heavy Metal in Baghdad* highlighted the practical and political difficulties of being in an underground band in a heavily militarised zone but Iran's freer system means while the political barriers aren't so strong, the financial ones are.

It's a similar story in the United Arab Emirates despite the presence of more tourist-dense areas like Abu Dabi and Dubai. In Abu Dabi in particular, there is a solitary Harley Davidson shop selling bikes and leathers mainly for the ex-pat community. Things are a little more relaxed in Turkey however where a small gothic music scene co-exists alongside darker metal styles like doom and death metal. It's likely the word 'gothic' holds little more relevance to the Turkish community as its architectural style can be spotted at various sites across the country and even former Bauhaus frontman Peter Murphy relocated to the country several years ago! Somewhat curiously a new craze for gothic belly dancing has crossed over from Turkey and into the US and parts of Europe, where you can learn how to perfect your wiggle courtesy of fellow goths via numerous DVDs.

Goth has also become part of the alternative scene in Israel and has been directly influenced and inspired by the movements out in Europe. "In the early '80s, people were going out on holiday to England and Western Europe and bringing back all this new and refreshing music with them," remembers local goth Yair. At the time the music scene was mainly dominated by local bands, many of whom had come from Tel Aviv's punk movement, the city that

Former Bauhaus frontman Peter Murphy is now living in Turkey © Pete Murphy

Teaming up with Israeli singer Ofra Haza, The Sisters Of Mercy found a new audience. © Per-Ake Warn

dictates trends in the small country. Gradually the first wave of goth emerged in Israel with gigs and clubs but it was short-lived as political turmoil in the area made foreign bands somewhat hesitant about playing there. By 1987, when goth was peaking in the UK, the Israeli–Palestinian conflict also reached a peak. New violence, including missile attacks and suicide bombings, made citizens extremely reluctant to leave their homes let alone go out to gigs and clubs so nothing more than a few underground events continued to run.

Despite the climate, the goth scene continued to send little ripples through popular culture, helped by Israeli pop singer Ofra Haza's vocal contributions to The Sisters Of Mercy's 1992 version of 'Temple Of Love', which gave the band a new audience in the country. These days, like elsewhere, the Israeli goth scene is split into several strands: there's the alternative/metal contingent, the EBM side and the more traditional gothic rock end of things with the music of popular European bands like Front 242, Bauhaus, Apoptygma Berzerk, and Clan of Xymox being played in Tel Aviv's gothic clubs and in the shops that sell gothic clothing. With a little more stability in the country, touring bands now go to play there again, mostly sticking to Tel Aviv and the surrounding larger towns of Haifa and Jerusalem. There are even a small number of local bands, including the gothic-metal doom inspired Distorted, who formed back in 1996 and have a European record deal with Candlelight, and the more industrial-orientated Death Made who are from the seaside city of Netanya. But the most striking aspect of all is that in Israel, goth is seen as an alternative subculture that's all about escapism. Devoid of its political roots and preferring to adopt a more low-key dress code, goth and punk in Israel preach music and fashion rather than anything else. Yair explains: "When we have events, politics are left outside the club – it's all about providing an environment that allows people to leave the stress of being in a country that's overrun by tension." Across the sea in Egypt another scene was starting to thrive, somewhat appropriately considering Egyptian symbols have always been popular in gothic culture – from the ankh, worn by Neil Gaiman's comic-book heroine Death, to the elaborate Eye of Horus that graced the cover of The Sisters Of Mercy's *Vision Thing*. The movement here is an offshoot of the metal and alternative scenes and, as with other areas of the Middle East, it operates underground without any nightclubs, local bands or alternative clothing stores. Contrary to assumptions that any kind of gothic look might blend in with a country it was so inspired by, many young alternative people have been arrested there for the way they look. Even though Western clothing is more commonplace in Egypt, very revealing styles of dress are still not acceptable for women and alternatively dressed men face accusations of homosexuality, which is considered to be "perverted" under local traditions and illegal under Sharia law. It certainly pales into insignificance the sort of verbal and physical abuse that many goths face from a prejudiced few and gives a very real reason for rebellion.

Similar scenes are gradually starting to appear via the metal scenes in Syria, Jordan, India and other nearby areas. There goth is often perceived as a more romantic side of metal that is obsessed with death and Victorian imagery and any arguments about goth and metal colliding would be met with confusion. The Lebanon even have their very own symphonic gothic metal band called Winter's Embrace. They formed towards the end of 2006, apparently inspired by the darker metal of touring bands like Theatre Of Tragedy.

In Pakistan, goth is similarly associated with metal and seems to have risen in popularity partly through the internet and partly because a large amount of mass-produced gothic clothing is manufactured in the area. At the time of writing, these scenes were so new that there were no local goth bands and few people had adopted the look although, if the popularity of Western heavy metal is anything to go by, it's likely to be only a matter of time before things change.

While gothic purists will argue these scenes have little in common with the original post-punk movement of the late '70s/early '80s, the simple fact is they do exist against all odds mainly thanks to the advent of the internet which has allowed music made even on a small scale to be enjoyed all around the world. In these countries, goth is as much about embracing a melancholic, darker side as it is rebelling against a strict system that sees anything alternative as a threat to law and order. The goth scene has always attracted those who felt like they didn't fit in with society – the outcasts, the poets, the geeky kids at school who were bullied for being different. While the sounds and fashions might alter slightly from country to country, and in some cases even within a single area, the appeal is still very much the same.

If further proof were needed, a slightly different strand of goth has spread

Outside the Elsinore at the Whitby Gothic Weekend, circa 1999
© Steve Godfrey

south from Canada and the US, down towards Mexico and South America. In Argentina's capital Buenos Aires, "darkies" started to appear in the early '80s although European bands like The Cure and Siouxsie And The Banshees didn't play there until the middle of the decade. The Argentinean post-punk movement gave birth to Euroshima, Art Noveau and Los Pillos to name but a few. Further south in Uruguay, RRRRRRR formed in 1987 and are recognised as being among the first gothic rock bands in the area. But as goth's popularity dwindled and metal became more prolific, a second wave came in via Germany in the 1990s thanks to a radio show called 'Testigos del Crepúsculo'. Presenter Mariano Cittadino played bands such as Lacrimosa, Umbra et Imago and Garden of Delight which further helped shape the scene and place the area on the map for underground touring bands.

But the new millennium helped shape the Buenos Aires scene further as American duo Fatal Beauties relocated in Argentina and brought their taste in contemporary US goth and deathrock with them. The music of Bella Morte, Fear Cult and Crüxshadows, all of which was also gaining popularity on the German scene, was being heard in South America and had a fair bit to do with the birth of the Bauhaus-inspired Brazilian goth band The Knutz. A few underground gothic events were held before the couple returned to the US leaving behind a legacy of new cultural references that were transformed into a portal called Gothic BA, which is now responsible for promoting gothic gigs, clubs and festivals across most of South America.

Brazil, Chile, Peru and Mexico are all part of this underground scene, the latter of which has become immersed with the annual Day Of The Dead celebrations – Mexico's version of Halloween. The gothic movement there has undergone quite a dramatic development over recent years as Lacrimosa frontman Tilo Wolff remembers: "The first time we went to Mexico in 1998, it was more like a metal scene there." But ten years later there's a huge gothic scene there. Keyboard player Anne Nurmi adds: "They were wearing metal t-shirts back then but now they have all the gothic clothing like we have here." The Mexican scene was also inspired by the emergence of electro-industrial in Europe and the US, which gave birth to the harsh electro-heads Hocico in the early '90s. Their music gave a harder, darker edge to what was in danger of becoming little more than a dance music scene while Brazilian bands such as Igreja Do Sexo (deathrock), Scarlet Leaves (darkwave), Seduced By Suicide (gothic rock) have since emerged. There's also Mexican gothic rockers Nietzsche's Bitch and the symphonic metal genre is also extremely popular in this area with bands like Nightwish playing large venues there.

LULL BEFORE THE STORM

It's hard to believe that a small youth movement that started back in the late '70s has grown into a worldwide subculture that perenially attracts all ages. Yet that is exactly what has happened to goth. Its focus has clearly changed, more so depending on which country you are in, yet it still uses the same identifiers and to the uninitiated bears many of the same trademarks. The blackened whirlpool of different genres that now makes up the goth scene (or not, depending on who you talk to!) help it to assimilate into a dramatic new musical movement with its own commercial weight.

By the end of the 20th century, there had been a huge shift of influence away from the UK scene – which had given birth to goth – towards other countries. By the turn of the millennium, a new version of goth worldwide would grow in popularity, although webzine editor Michael Johnson muses: "There's probably some sort of equation here: the further you get in space and time from the source, the more people try to define the source. And the less they get it right!"

Whether "right" or not, Goth's profile was on the up but in April 1999, something happened in a suburban area of Colorado that caused ripples throughout the scene and raised goth's public image in a rather negative way. Two American teenagers went on a killing spree at their high school in Denver, Colorado, killing 13 people and injuring many others before committing suicide. The media caught onto the story of the Columbine Massacre and incorrectly reported that Dylan Klebold and Eric Harris were goths and members of a society called The Trenchcoat Mafia. Bands such as KMFDM, Rammstein and Marilyn Manson were all named in the media with the implication they were somehow responsible for tipping the pair over the edge but as more evidence was found, it was discovered that neither killer had anything to do with the gothic subculture nor any interest in the alternative bands mentioned. Yet the damage had already been done and many religious groups took it as a sign that this music and fashion subculture was an evil cult that was somehow caught up with Satanism. Their evidence was seemingly reinforced in 2002 by a murder case in Germany where a British goth club was mentioned as being the venue of blood-drinking parties. Although it became apparent during the case that no such events had in fact taken place, a number of goths were contacted by journalists trying to find out more. German electronic act :wumpscut: even wrote a song about the case called simply 'Ruda', which related to the way in which the German media had linked the goth and industrial scenes to Satanism.

Further controversy was stirred up when some mainstream media organisations accused certain goth bands of flirting with Nazi imagery, particularly in the neo-folk movement. The charge was roundly denied but again, damage was done – the bad press has given rise to a Goths Against Nazis (Grufties Gegen Nazis) movement in Germany that keeps an eye on things.

Media ignorance and scaremongering among certain religious groups in the US haven't helped the situation either and one source even claims that goths wear white foundation because they're all white supremacists! Given the punk movement's anarchic tendencies, it was surely only a matter of time before goth got tarnished with a more political brush and religious campaigners can often be spotted leafleting large gatherings of goths at dark music festivals like Wave Gotik Treffen and M'era Luna. To those on the outside though, it seems almost unthinkable that a peaceful and creative subculture like goth could even be associated with such extreme political views.

Nadine, formerly with Montreal goth band Bordello. © Stephane Lord www.darkfairies.co.uk

REBiRTH

"Is that still going on?" Siouxsie Sioux asked

with a hesitant laugh when I spoke to her about goth in an interview for *meltdown* magazine back in 2002. There are few movements that can genuinely claim to still be gathering momentum more than thirty years after they first crept into youth culture. While some parts of today's goth scene are unrecognisable from their punk origins, other elements have been reborn and strengthened for what has now become a worldwide subculture. "It's the similarities [in the goth scenes across the world] that are the most striking to me," explains The Specimen and former Banshees' guitarist Jon Klein. "Imagine you're driving through the deserted hills of Italy and in the middle of nowhere there is a group of Robert Smiths in long black coats walking single file on the open road!"

The word 'gothic' was always meant to be ambiguous and that's what has helped its dark aesthetic continue to thrive and be picked up on, not to mentioned be redefined by new generations. Goth has changed dramatically in the last thirty years from its original semi-political musical roots and individual DIY look to something more Romantic, slightly sinister with often very expensive clothing that follows a Victoriana theme. It's frequently meshed with different and seemingly contrasting musical styles although glimmers of its early ethos still crop up around parts of Europe, the UK and the US.

Siouxsie Sioux © Fiona Freud

But as reinvention is often the key to success, it can also hinder development as Michael 'Uncle Nemesis' Johnson noticed: "By the time the 21st century rolled around, goth in the UK had taken a bit of a dip again. It wasn't the same kind of scenario as the early 1990s: then, the basic problem was that aside from sporadic chart hits by a handful of mainstream-friendly crossover stars, there simply wasn't much goth stuff going on at all. That was not the problem in the 2000s – there was quite a lot of activity in goth circles. But by this time the UK goth scene had essentially become a social scene, rather than a music scene. That was the problem… If you look at the London goth scene today,

Italian goth Michela
© Stephane Lord www.darkfairies.co.uk

that's what it is: an entire social whirl of shopping and clubbing, picnics and outings, trips to the cinema and museums. It's always busy, always lively [and there's] always something going on. But gigs fit into all this only insofar as they provide another social space. Another reason to meet up with friends and go out and have fun. Fair enough – but there isn't a huge amount of interest in music for its own sake."

Goth's shifting ethos meant that while certain subgenres were flourishing, others were starting to become obsolete and even a bit cliquey. Live music might have been slowly in decline but clubs and other social activities were on the increase turning the goth scene away from its musical roots and closer towards the image side of things. All this had a rather noticeable effect on the sort of mainstream press coverage the genre was giving it and regardless of the role of the internet, the majority of fans still need some guidance. "I don't think the media can decide whether or not goth is passé," says artist Anne Sudworth. She adds: "The coverage of goth music varies a lot, though coverage of music genres is always on the move…[but] there have been numerous attempts to do features on goth culture, I'd say more so in the last few years. We've had everything from goth lifestyle features to goths in soaps. I've had several enquiries this year as to whether I'd take part in some sort of TV reality show or other such thing, to all of which I've said no. [I think] goth as a scene seems to fall in and out of favour with the general media on a regular basis."

Since the murder of gothic student Sophie Lancaster in 2007, goth as a subculture seems to be back in favour with

Artist Anne Sudworth
© Darren Andrews

UK media. The pro-gothic coverage given to the case seems to have reduced the number of unprovoked attacks on goths in many parts of the UK and the S.O.P.H.I.E. campaign [Stamp Out Prejudice Hatred and Intolerance Everywhere] is still running to this day (the official site can be found at www.sophielancasterfoundation.com).

Despite appearances, there was still plenty of music being made however. As technology has become cheaper and the internet faster and more reliable as a source of very cheap self-promotion, there are a huge amount of new gothic and goth-inspired bands out there all over the world. Webzines and online communities gradually superseded all those paper fanzines that worked as the essential thread connecting the worldwide gothic scene over the previous decades. Even ready-made gothic clothing had become not only easy to locate online but could also be found on the high street.

Against this background, the UK underground goth movement was continuing to tick away quite merrily. Although the synthesis from post-punk to gothic rock and more electronic styles that it experienced in the '90s helped to create new interest in the scene, it was reluctant to absorb the external influences that other European scenes had. Electronic and cybergoth styles were still very popular, along with the obligatory glo-sticks and neon accessories. In 2000, Front Line Assembly side-project Delerium even hit the top three in the official UK chart with 'Silence' which momentarily threatened to put goth on the mainstream map for a while. The synthesis of the electronic movement within the goth scene was felt in other countries too. "I think people [here] are influenced more by what they idealise the international scenes as being," Z00g from Australian cyberpunk duo Angelspit explains. "Cybergoth was huge in London but around 2003 the craziest cybergoth was in Sydney ... it was insane! We grew out of [its] height in 2004! We try and take the flamboyance of the Australian cybergoth scene but musically and visually [we're] more hard."

Electronic music has also held fast in Scotland's goth scene. Back in the early days, Aberdeen's goth movement was a rather hybrid affair as Elizium club's clientele crossed over with the city's horror punk and rockabilly contingent. Regular 'Reck and Roll' nights were being run by Ash and Michelle from local alternative fashion store Retro Rebels (now home to the Kreepsville 666

Australian duo Angelspit, who now live in the US.
© Angelspit

brand of horror punk couture) and the cross-promotion of gigs and other events kept both pulses beating. By the early 2000s though, the music got faster and more electronic causing quite a change in its cross-pollination. Promoter Alun Hughes remembers: "By 2002 we were running Elizium at Dr Drakes and it was pretty much packed out every night. The audience was radically different, with the goth element down to serious classics and some modern stuff as long as it had 'punch'. We'd stolen music from the electroclash scene – Fischerspooner or Felix Da Housecat [were] nestled in amongst Covenant and Apoptygma Berzerk. The 'old school' element was pretty much industrial – Skinny Puppy, Ministry, Pigface etc all still worked with our clientele. [But] glo-sticks were out, club looks slowly infiltrated and there was something of a resurgence in the dark alt scene; but it definitely wasn't a 'goth' club anymore. To be honest, from multi-club events like The Nightmare Afore Christmas run in Edinburgh, the feeling I got was the whole of Scotland was, by this time, heavily in to the bleep [aka electronic dance music] and EBM – or at least that's the direction most clubs seemed to be pushing in. Aside from a few old die-hard goths, we had the younger generation populating our club, so we played to them and what was new … we found fringe stuff from the punky, electro sound to our liking; we put on bands like Motormark, The Kitchen [featuring Amanda from indie band Bis) and Japan's Psydoll, or Covenant in Edinburgh. Trad goth was, to us, pretty much gone up here in Aberdeen." The latest carnation of the club is pretty much full-on electro-industrial and even the playlists for Edgar's new Snakebite goth night lean heavily towards electronic music.

But down south, there was more of a pull towards the traditional gothic rock sound with bleep-free bands like The Faces Of Sarah, Voices Of Masada and a revised version of All Living Fear starting to emerge. This paved the way for a mini deathrock and horror punk explosion a few years later that saw the goth scene once again partnered with punk rather than metal. Michael Johnson retired from gig promotion and Flag Promotions joined the goth scene even though they had already been promoting events on the electronic side of the fence for a while. GOG Promotions in Leeds, the Insanitarium crew in Colchester, Cardiff's Necroscope and Reading's SoGoth/Church Of Madness team who were behind the short-lived Malediction festival were among some of the other prolific UK underground gig promoters at the time. Some key venues like Birmingham's Mercat had closed but new nights were on the increase from London's very own deathrock club Dead And Buried to Cambridge's Sacrilege and The Calling, Newcastle-Upon-Tyne's Charnel House, York's Darklands, Preston's Dark-Cide, The Coven in Luton and Oxford's Intrusion. All this existed without any help from the mainstream press, although zines such as *Kaleidoscope* and *meltdown* were key components of an underground network of small press.

Independent record labels also continued to play a part and Wasp Factory was set up in the early '00s initially as a medium for the electronic band The Chaos Engine to release their music but would eventually sign a host of edgy new acts. Frontman Lee Chaos remembers: "We played the Whitby Gothic Weekend in April 2000 alongside VNV Nation, Mesh and Sigue Sigue Sputnik. There was an interesting mix of dark electronic and more traditional goth music. There were also, as I recall, a lot of complaints from goths that the music was not goth. In my opinion this was the beginning of the end."

He continues: "[Bradford's Industrial festival] Infest started in 1998 but really hit its stride in 2001. It effectively split the UK scene into two and separated the electronic and EBM bands from the more traditional goth fare. For a scene that seems to spend so much time pontificating about how alternative it is, I think it's ironic that such a narrow-minded outlook towards what constituted goth music resulted in many of the more interesting acts being absorbed by what was ostensibly a rival event. You don't see that in Europe so much and I think the scene is more vibrant as a direct result."

Wasp Factory helped put British goth music back on the map of credibility out in Europe as Chaos and Brighton alternative music promoter Mark 'Eris' Firman concentrated on grabbing bands who they felt were not only capable of writing great material but who were also able to present it in an interesting way. "We weren't looking for the next Cure or the next Nine Inch Nails, we were looking for something new with each signing and I think sometimes that put us a little too far ahead for people to easily understand," he explains. The result was that the label had a very eclectic feel with samplers that included acts as diverse as industrial noise merchants Leechwoman nestling alongside the dreamier synth-pop of Swarf. Chaos sighs: "The mainstream media are always looking for the Next Big Thing – their narrative is about moving forwards, not backwards. Goths, to the media, are a curio in the same way as you might see punks on postcards in London [so] Wasp Factory more or less existed in a bubble for the first four or five years of operation. We certainly had no delusions about trying to change media's opinions towards goth music... we often found it hard to be taken seriously because of

Sid from Dream Disciples © Steve Godfrey

our affiliation with the goth scene. [But] abroad we found that publications were appreciably more open-minded."

Although the label eventually ceased, Wasp Factory's ethos of credibility did raise the bar and reminded the rest of Europe that the UK was still capable of producing good quality alternative music that didn't always sound like the generic 'Sisters-Of-The-Nephilim' output that the latter part of the '90s had been so guilty of. In Scotland, former Dream Disciples frontman Col Lowing briefly tried a similar approach with Darkcell Digital Music and in the Antipodes, something called the Crash Frequency Collective was born in 2004 which continues to help raise the profile of darker bands out in Australia and New Zealand. Within a few years, many of the UK goth scene's bands from the 1990s had been merged into new ones and a more traditional approach to the sound had been resurrected along with The Sisters' drum machine sound. Rhombus, Legion, The Ghost of Lemora, Pretentious, Moi? (featuring members of Dream Disciples and Manuskript) and Grooving In Green (with previous members of '90s band Children On Stun) all re-created that faithful sound. That said, more new electronic bands are also still emerging like Deviant UK, Method Cell and the more hybrid Last July and Miserylab (featuring Rosetta Stone's Porl King).

But it's the more traditional gothic rock sound that has become regarded as something of a template that many new bands adhere to. Its popularity seems to wax and wane with sudden peaks and troughs of old-school sounding bands throughout the years and there are those who have even tried to break free from that tried-and-tested gothic formula by cross-referencing more unexpected influences in their music with varying levels of success. Amongst them, a more compact version of Screaming Banshee Aircrew, The Eden House (featuring Tony Pettitt from Fields Of The Nephilim), Adoration (featuring former London promoter John Banshee) and In Isolation (featuring former members of Emma Conquest and Die Laughing). While many have won themselves new fans in the process, Screaming Banshee Aircrew in particular sometimes found themselves stuck at the half-way point of being too goth for an indie crowd but too indie for the goth scene, which eventually contributed to their dissolution in 2010. Interestingly Zeraphine from Germany and France's Les Modules Etranges follow a similar musical path that isn't regarded at odds with their respective scenes although both have yet to make an impact on the UK.

The Irish scene – both Northern and the Republic – has remained more of a mixed bag with a close-knit network. DiscMistress Tracey runs Belfast's Cornucopia night and explains: "Belfast and Dublin are the only places there are regular goth events – [we] try to support each other whenever [we] can. I run coaches to Ministry of Agroculture Promotions gigs and Dominion Club in Dublin, where I've guest DJ'ed many times [and] DJs from Dublin often come and play at my club too. There are [intermittent] events in Derry, Cork and other cities ... I guess the problem is transport and costs so it makes more sense for events to be on where it's easiest for people to get to and where the most people live." Wales has a similarly close-knit scene these days with the Cardiff's goth/industrial/electro night Inquisition being the main attraction.

CHANGING FACES

There was one key event that did have an impact on the resurgence of the goth scene in the early '00s although it had little effect on the underground scene itself. In 2003 another attempt to take goth mainstream was made but it had little to do with the sound or look that had been made popular two decades previously. Arkansas band Evanescence shot to number one in the British charts with their nu-metal single 'Bring Me To Life', which scored them major recognition around the world. Their album *Fallen*, released through Sony subsidiary Wind Up, bore many of the hallmarks of the gothic metal style that was becoming more and more popular in Europe while the band's image – particularly that of frontwoman Amy Lee who made a lot of her own outfits – contributed towards the changing face of gothic fashion.

As interest was raised in Evanescence, so the profile of gothic metal also peaked with the likes of Lacuna Coil, Nightwish, Within Temptation, Type O

Negative and even Paradise Lost crossing over to a much younger market. Marilyn Manson and the Finnish glam-metal band HIM also got a look in but whether they were real goth or not seems to remain a moot point because the simple fact is that all these bands raised more interest in gothic culture. This fusion also contributed to an unexpected development that took place in Italy at the turn of the 21st century when two new gothic bands took a great deal of inspiration from that Finnish scene. Bloody Mary formed in 2000 and borrowed the whole goth 'n' roll image and sound – their 2005 debut album was called simply *Blood N Roll*. In 2002 in Rome, singer-songwriter Victor Love had decided to swap his glam rock roots for something a little more electronic and formed a new band called Dope Stars Inc. He'd been spending a lot of time in Helsinki and ended up mixing industrial rock with gothic metal to create a rather catchy style that was matched with a striking pretty boy image. The band's debut album *Neuromance* was produced by Thomas Rainer from Austrian darkwave-electro band L'Âme Immortelle and John Fryer, who has been name-checked on influential releases by Cocteau Twins, Fields Of The Nephilim and Nine Inch Nails to name but a few. It was a winning formula which carried onto the self-styled 'Tokyo pop' sound of their

second offering *Gigahearts* even though guitarist Alex Vega left the band in 2007 to develop his gothic doom metal band known as The Foreshadowing. Love has since become a much sought-after producer and is currently working on a heavier industrial-rock sound with his side-project Epochate. As for Dope Stars Inc, they're still active and have since notched up a reasonable fanbase not just in their home country but also in the UK, Finland, Russia and Japan. Were it not for them, it's possibly unlikely that fellow Italian electro-rock influenced bands such as Latexxx Teens (featuring singer Krimloth from black metallers Draconian Order) and the saccharine-sweet sounding

The sugar-coated Helalyn Flowers © Helalyn Flowers

Italy's Bloody Mary © Valery Records

Helalyn Flowers would have come along in their wake. "These days, the Italian Goth audience is most interested in EBM, electro-goth and industrial," explains Max from Helalyn Flowers. "Dope Stars Inc and us were responsible for the cross between gothic rock /metal and industrial [that] exploded back in 2005 – [the scene] is full of club-goers now who are most interested in dancing." The Lovecrave and Macbeth have since joined Italy's gothic metal roster and, although first appearances suggest this mish-mash of bands must surely have nothing in common, the promoter Sebastian Rizza from Alter Arts Agency explains this isn't necessarily the case: "Many people from the metal scene have started to get interested in the more electronic goth movement here as well. For example, concerts by

Norway's Mortiis and his live band © Mortiis

harder electronic bands like Hocico, Suicide Commando and Combichrist have actually been very popular with metal fans too and that's helped raise numbers in the goth scene."

DJ BMC agrees: "Italy's dark movement has sort of oddly blended with metal now, partly due to venues like Transilvania [in Milan] offering a wide range of events in the same night and mixing audiences. It's not unusual to find people with quite an eclectic taste in music nowadays…"

The problem was, of course, that once again goth had become fashionable and once again, as soon as the bubble burst, interest waned and numbers

dropped. Add this to the natural shedding of older goths in the underground movement and there was quite a marked decline in the scene by the mid-'00s. In some parts of Europe, many gothic metal followers became absorbed into the hard rock and metal scenes while out in Germany, the multi-faceted Schwarze Szene was able to re-assimilate them into different pockets of dark culture, albeit at the expense of the original goth scene. In fact, it was most probably that assimilation process that made it easy for bands like Crematory and Norway's Mortiis and Gothminister to change musical styles across albums.

While the internet was still continuing to play a very important role in both the hybrid and underground goth scenes by around 2004, newsgroups had waned in popularity and been replaced by blogs, then MySpace and Last.fm followed by Facebook and Twitter – all just as important as each other in promoting not only underground gothic music but also events and businesses all around the world. The problem was, so many cyber-resources meant the online goth scene was more spread out than it had been two decades ago and this meant that against all appearances, it wasn't as well-connected. And to add further irony to the mix, the bigger goth became online the smaller its physical presence was in the real world. In fact the very thing that was goth's lifeline in the '90s ended up sticking it on a life support machine a decade later!

But all the while, there was something else rather interesting beginning to happen that had absolutely nothing to do with this underground scene. The early days of British post-punk were being revived as part of a new movement that bore all the hallmarks of goth, including that ubiquitous element of self-denial! It started off with the raw garage rock of American bands like The Strokes and White Stripes and transformed into something much darker through Dragons, The Editors, Interpol and more recently White Lies. The *NME* were embracing what they referred to as "nu gloom" in the issue cover-dated 28 February 2009, but this "new" scene had actually already been evolving for several years.

It was roughly around 2005 when the metamorphosis began, almost as a simultaneous reaction against the nu, or new rave scene. "Nu rave" was a joke term coined by indie label Angular Records co-founder Joe Daniel to describe a type of indie music that borrowed elements from the Madchester rave scene and modernised them with a fresh sound. Daniel was a former student at Goldsmiths University in New Cross and it was along that stretch of East London's overground line that the new post-punk scene spread and ironically earned itself the nu grave moniker. Angular signees The Violets and The Horrors, who found themselves caught up in the whole emo craze, were among the first bands to be part of the movement. The Violets' sound was not dissimilar to Siouxsie And The Banshees with their staccato vocals and angular guitars, while The Horrors from Southend-on-Sea initially drew their musical inspiration from The Birthday Party and Bauhaus and their look from Manchester punk performance poet John Cooper Clarke, attracting crowds of trendy young-things who imitated their back-combed hair, skinny jeans and winkle pickers. Their first gig was at a self-promoted night in the Shoreditch/Hoxton area of East London – a neighbourhood made popular by artists and designers because of the cheap rents at the time. They continued to run frequent nights between London and Southend, which helped an actual scene come together. Appearances on the comedy series *The Mighty Boosh* along with similarly dark acts like IAMX and Gary Numan further helped raise their profile.

The mainstream media might have considered goth music unfashionable but soon those seminal dark bands from the '80s started to end up in student MP3 collections and their punky looks were recreated with vintage clothing and lots of black eyeliner. A number of new bands fell out of this burgeoning Shoreditch scene, among them SCUM, Ipso Facto, Silhouette, Eve White/Eve Black (who later changed their name to An Experiment On A Bird In The Air Pump) and Neils Children. Their angular and occasionally raucous sounds contrasted the safer indie-electronic sounds that nu rave bands like The Klaxons, New Young Pony Club and Shitdisco were pushing around the clubs and in fact, several of the bands who would later become part of this new dark indie movement had originally started off with an electronic sound. "I'd been banging a drum and carrying a torch for the post-punk aesthetic for years without much result and without much interest from anyone else," says Michael Johnson. "Now at last it was all happening… [but] the goth scene didn't even notice it…it was as if goth had forgotten where it had come from." Johnson began covering this new movement first on the alternative webzine *Starvox* and then on his own *Nemesis To Go* site, which was often visited by those who remembered his days as a London goth gig promoter. He coined the term "non-scene" to describe this new movement, distinguishing it from the underground gothic events that were still taking place regardless.

Word spread around this new post-punk scene and more nights opened – the underground magazine *Artrocker* even put its name to several as its pages were filled with articles about these new bands, many of whom didn't last very long. The scene even hit the tabloids via Peaches Geldof first when she briefly became part of This Tawdry Affair – the band continued without her, regardless of a reduced amount of media attention – and then when her dad Sir Bob pulled her up over her favourite offensively-named band Bono Must Die. Festivals like 1234 and Offset pulled bands such as Romance and Ulterior away from dingy basements and into the sunlight. While in the mainstream Florence And The Machine (featuring former Ipso Facto keyboardist Cherish Kaya) became prolific in the charts and US songstress Zola Jesus mixed the

O Children – the new face of goth? © Deadly People

DeadlyDoll & Azadeh from RazorBladeKisses
©Stephane Lord www.darkfairies.co.uk

New Fiction signees Romance © Dean Chalkley

Faith And The Muse © Danse Macabre

eeriness of the Cocteau Twins in her sound. Wheels had been set in motion and were gathering momentum so it was only a matter of time before the new post-punk scene became merged with the old one. The Violets and Ipso Facto both got booked to support Siouxsie Sioux for consecutive years of her solo tour, Ulterior supported both The Sisters Of Mercy and UK Decay and The Cure's Robert Smith teamed up with nu ravers Crystal Castles. Two previous members of Bono Must Die formed a new band that took their less controversial name from a Nick Cave And The Bad Seeds song. O Children earned themselves a lot of rather justified comparisons to Joy Division with their self-titled debut album and single 'Dead Disco Dancer' which ended up on the in-store playlist for high street chain TopShop, while Romance found themselves snapped up by Polydor's Fiction label (the same one The Cure had been signed to) and went out on the road with their '80s heroes The Cult. Johnson comments: "There's definitely a similar feeling in the air to the early '80s – a feeling that you can push the creative boat out and catch a following wind. It's been a long time since we've had that." A handful of bands have since been brought over to the underground goth movement and others have made in-roads at crossing over to that dark indie scene including Luxury Stranger and Hiram Key. In Isolation are another as frontman Ryan Swift, formerly of Emma Conquest explains: "My own vision was to draw on the earlier '80s post-punk sounds but I also liked the more popular new wave tracks which often filled the 'normal' charts at the same time. I thought we could bridge the gap between the two, but also take influence from general 'indie' musical developments which had occurred in the subsequent twenty-odd years."

Of the new Shoreditch scene, he says: "I don't think it has really found its way properly out of London yet. A lot of these newer bands are capturing the essence of some of the early '80s bands [and] it's quite an exciting time. There seems to be quite an attitude to some of them too, harking back to the earlier post-punk days [which is] another winner."

It's been strange to watch these darker bands, whose music is so close to the scene that goth originally came from, being pushed by a media that mocked the g-word for so long. While those in the newer scenes might associate goth with something beautiful and mysterious, in the scenes where it's been going for longer it's still associated with some very bizarre things. "The term 'goth' is never going to be taken seriously," says In Isolation's frontman Ryan Swift. "The British media's fascination with sensationalism has been prevalent for quite some time – any tabloid story which has alluded to the word 'goth' has included the likes of grannies with fangs or Satan-worshipping deviants. There is too much ridicule attached to the word for it to ever be considered worthy of credibility in the commercial world."

But this backdrop of 'dark indie' worship cleared the path for '80s bands like Bauhaus, Siiiii, Skeletal Family, March Violets, Vendemmian and The

Chameleons to reform. Their retro sound, often revamped for the live show with modern equipment, went down a storm in the UK and also out in Europe where they were welcomed as the traditional sound of goth. Even Fields Of The Nephilim, Killing Joke and Siouxsie And The Banshees reformed, albeit with slightly different line-ups.

Siouxsie in particular had been experimenting with different sounds with her side-project The Creatures, which was resurrected with her then-husband Budgie towards the end of the '90s. *Anima Animus* focused on the electronic music scene but its follow-up *Hai!* returned to the tribal drumming format that played a large role in the duo's music. The Creatures married Eastern culture with the West by bringing in the Kodo drummers – a group of traditional Japanese musicians with a very distinctive sound. This marriage was also revisited by US band Faith And The Muse's 2009 album *Ankoku Butoh,* which used traditional taiko drums that brought an extra layer of darkness to their beautiful music.

Japanese influence popped up elsewhere in the goth scene as visual kei and gothic lolita styles spread across the world, first through computer games and then through conventions. It was here that cosplay started to become part of gothic culture in Europe, Australia and the US. *The Gothic & Lolita Bible* was eventually translated into English, with US and European editions now available. Meanwhile Gan-Shin Records was set up in Germany to deal with the distribution of bands like Dir En Grey, the UK got its very first EGL band called Razorbladekisses and the scene is now quite large in parts of Scandinavia and France, where Europe's biggest Japanese convention has been held for the last decade. Some of this Japanese gothic influence filtered across into the metal scene where its mix of cute and dark brought new followers to the scene. Ironically the scene is far less popular now in Japan. Many visual kei bands like Dir En Grey and L'Arc-en-Ciel have moved away from the genre, and the Jrock

Mana – the gothfather of Elegant Gothic Lolita now runs his own fashion label.
(c) Gan-Shin Records

musical style they were once part of has now become a bigger commercial movement mostly filled with manufactured pop bands. "It just got to a point where we felt constricted by our costumes. And we also lost the passion for wearing what we used to ..." Dir En Grey's Kaoru admits of their current metal status. What was once alternative is now quite mainstream and the same is true for the gothic lolita style, which is now more of a fashion than an indication of musical taste. Against this background, the underground label Darkest Labyrinth has expanded its roster to include the Japanese Seileen and GPKISM (Kiwamu from BLOOD's dark electronic side-project) as well as licensing acts like Australia's harsh electro duo Angelspit and Italy's Spectrum X. The addition of bands from other countries shows that while the underground goth scene may not be as popular in Japan as previously, it still has an international

Alt model Fracture © Martin Small

appeal. Deathwatch Asia's Jamie Nova admits the local Jgoth scene is somewhat stagnant at the moment with those homegrown bands doing better abroad than on their home turf. Admittedly some darker international acts do draw crowds – IAMX, Dope Stars Inc and Alien Vampires are among them – but it's the Elegant Gothic Lolita (EGL) style that seems to have outlived the music and spread outside the Far East to some very unexpected locations.

Nearby China and Malaysia seem to have been slow to catch on with little evidence of a goth scene in either location. However the lolita style is now starting to appear in Hong Kong, which has also been slow on the uptake with the gothic scene only really starting to emerge in the last few years. Tilo Wolff from the German/Finnish Lacrimosa remembered when he played in Taiwan in 2007: "I think we were the first goth band over there... There were all these normal business people in front of the venue. I thought there was no audience yet so I could go out for a coffee but suddenly all these men in their suits and ties got out their Lacrimosa albums and I realised that gothicks look like that here because they don't know what to wear yet."

But despite all this, the West's take on EGL fits perfectly with what violin maestro Emilie Autumn was working on in Chicago. Emilie Autumn started her career in the classical arena but quickly got bored of its insular nature so

Violinist Emilie Autumn
© Michael Johnson

started working as a solo artist and guest musician in the alternative realm. She's clocked up credits working with Billy Corgan from Smashing Pumpkins, Courtney Love from Hole and UK underground gothic band Avoidance Of Doubt. "I was a melancholy, death-obsessed child with night-terrors ... I've actually lightened up a lot as I've grown older!" she reveals. But her solo breakthrough came around 2006 when she merged her classically virtuoso violin sound with goth and industrial to create 'violindustrial'. At that time, she was unsigned but managed to create a presence on MySpace and attracted a large fanbase who were mesmerised by her strong lolita image and catchy tunes. She was signed to Trisol Records who released her debut *Opheliac* and quickly the Emilie Autumn show started touring in as many places as humanly possible.

But this wasn't a rock show, this was pure cabaret. Elements of burlesque – which had been creeping into gothic culture via the LA fetish scene and got twisted up with the European psychobilly movement – were brought out to play along with the terribly English idea of tea and crumpets. Drawing on her own experiences of mental health treatment (she frequently talks about her bi-polar diagnosis), the Emilie Autumn show is set in a mock Victorian mental asylum with its inmates – Autumn's backing troupe the Bloody Crumpets – telling stories of their life through her songs. Baked goods are flung out to her

Emilie Autumn and the Bloody Crumpets live in London
© Taya Uddin

fans, who are referred to as Muffins and often imitate her hand-made costumes just as the visual kei fans practiced cosplay with their favourite bands. The whole experience leans closer towards Alice Cooper's elaborate Theatre Of Death than The Sisters Of Mercy but there was still something intrinsically dark about her music and image. Her songs, which flit between darkwave and neo-classical, have even been remixed for the dancefloor by artists such as Dope Stars Inc and ASP making them fit quite neatly with the electronic-rock sound of the US underground scene alongside Crüxshadows and The Last Dance. Autumn has since become something of a role model for depressed teenagers, offering words of hope and encouragement through interviews and her book *The Asylum For Wayward Victorian Girls* which contains entries from the diaries she kept while receiving psychiatric treatment.

Whether her followers agree on her being goth or not is irrelevant because her message is quite clear: "I don't choose my audience, they choose me … and I respect them for it," she says. "I didn't do market research … and if anyone needs to see my street cred, they're free to review my scars, my shrink's records of my suicide attempts, and my charts from the insane asylum. I'm not ashamed of them. But seriously, if that ain't goth, I don't know what is…" More recently, her look has perhaps started to veer towards a rather curious movement called steampunk, which seems to have unwittingly joined the gothic party.

BACK TO THE FUTURE

"Steampunk is the new goth," explains Drew Bernstein from LA alternative clothing company Lip Service, as he reveals it's one of their most popular current ranges. "The look is more Victoriana with corsets and waist-lines and bustles and these puffy princess sleeves …"

Steampunk first came about as a literature genre in the 1980s – it was the tongue-in-cheek opposite of the term 'cyberpunk', the genre made popular by writers Bruce Bethke and William Gibson. Although a fashion movement briefly emerged via the successful film *Blade Runner*, cyberpunk's futuristic implications were mostly absorbed into the cybergoth sub-genre. Steampunk, however, seems to have taken on a life of its own as a modern take on days gone by.

Influenced by the age of the steam train, steampunk fits comfortably with gothic fashion's Victorian trend but instead of the funereal black velvets and silver jewellery, brown tweed, leather and brass pieces, often based around clock parts and complicated invention pieces are hugely popular. Part-re-enactor and part-fashion, steampunk appears to have slowly crept out of the world of book and comic conventions towards the end of the '90s and early

Steampunk hits Germany's Wave Gotik Treffen. © Stephen Milward

Andy Heintz and Andrew O'Neill from
The Men That Will Not Be Blamed For Nothing © Tim Sutton

Simon Satori from Rome Burns © Martin Small

Alternative model AndromedaX
© Julian M. Kilsby

2000s. There's even the variant Western steampunk, which isn't a million miles away from what Fields Of The Nephilim themselves were doing back in the early '80s.

But steampunk isn't just about dressing up and going to various conventions, it's also spawned a musical style of its own! At the more gothic end of the spectrum bands like Abney Park and Ghostfire mix modern darkwave with an eclectic selection of hand-made and very old fashioned-looking instruments, while The Men That Will Not Be Blamed For Nothing take a slightly different approach. This more light-hearted band have more in-keeping with the post-punk sound and feature Andy Heintz from '80s gothic metal band Creaming Jesus as well as alt comedian Andrew O'Neill. "We formed as a musical extension of Andrew's Edinburgh show *The Spot-on History Of British Industry*," explains Heintz. "[We were] trying to imagine what a punk band formed in the 1880s would sound like and what subjects they would sing about … looking around we found a whole scene of like-minded creative people with a love of similar aesthetics and a wonderful DIY culture, which we fitted snugly into!"

Edwardian-themed dark cabaret outfit Tiger Lillies (who have worked with The Banshees' Steven Severin), illustrator-cum-singer-songwriter Voltaire and the duo Dresden Dolls have more recently been finding themselves lumped into the steampunk category for their more eclectic sound and unusual performances. In terms of inventiveness, steampunk is comparable to what has been going on with the medieval/mittelalter scene in Germany – in fact, there's already a regional variation of steampunk in the eastern part of the country, which is called Preußen Punk. From the outside, it might look the same but its followers take themselves far more seriously with for example more authentic materials being used so their accessories are in fully-working order rather than just decorative plastic.

More recently the steampunk style has been merged with other gothic sub-genres, like gothic lolita, and is becoming assimilated within the goth scenes out in Europe, the US and even Australia. Z00g from Aussie cyberpunk band Angelspit explains: "Steampunk is currently huge [in the US] but the most innovative stuff I've seen has been from Australia and New Zealand. I think there's a drive in Australia to out-do [everywhere else]!?"

But it's not the only nostalgic trend in the goth scene because psychobilly has also gone back to its roots with rockabilly and burlesque fashions returning to the contemporary goth scene. These were key influences back in the days of punk where teddy boy jackets, known as drapes, and brothel creeper shoes were key parts of the look. Burlesque performer and model Dita Von Teese has certainly played a role in popularising the look, not just in the goth scene but also in more mainstream fashion, although her influence is certainly not exclusive.

It seems like goth has come almost in a full circle and the revival of deathrock should also not be ignored. It began as a backlash against the growing popularity of electronic music within gothic culture towards the end of the 1990s. While gothic rock was making a comeback in the UK's underground scene, in the US deathrock was being merged with the post-punk sounds of the Batcave to create a new old-school sound that played on its early rock 'n' roll influences but kept away from goth's more thoughtful art-school aesthetic. The big hair and war paint of the '80s made a return and clubs with a "no EBM" policy started to emerge.

One of the first bands to rekindle this style was California's Cinema Strange. "We got started near Los Angeles in 1994," muses frontman Lucas Lanthier. "I remember a pretty confused scene at that time. While there were a few mohicans running about, they were a rare thing, there was a lot of crushed velvet,

Lucas Lanthier from Cinema Strange and The Deadfly Ensemble
© Stephane Lord www.darkfairies.co.uk

London deathrocker Matt
© Stephane Lord www.darkfairies.co.uk

poet shirts and Fabio pirate pants on display and significantly a growing EBM movement, so to speak. Suffice to say, when we started playing shows we stuck out like a gangrenous toe on the rubber-sandaled foot of a beachfront prostitute! It took a while for people to catch on… I think we were playing shows for about five years before people started really paying attention [but] I'm glad they eventually did. Maybe we just stuck around long enough for the scene to change and make us fashionable! We grabbed lots of things from the old LA deathrock scene and the old Batcave scene in London and we mixed them up with our own bizarre sense of musical art and went for a one-band revival. I think part of the thrill, however, was doing something totally different. I know that the more we started seeing mohawks and fishnet stockings, the more we started experimenting with costumes and set pieces. I remember that for one of the WGT festivals in Leipzig, we went anti-Batcave, wearing pastels and floral prints and we had a sunny, flowery backdrop. Of course, we also had bloody-stumped decapitated stuffed animals that were regularly kicked out into the audience, but overall it was a very 'tea-time on Easter' sort of show."

As Cinema Strange's revolt started to get them noticed, other bands joined the party. Diva Destruction, Antiworld and Element were gathering a lot of interest with a newly developed deathrock style while older bands like Voodoo Church and 45 Grave gradually reformed and Eva O – Rozz Williams' former partner and Shadow Project collaborator – resurrected her career with a new band and new material. Slowly but surely word spread and more bands began to appear from outside the US and the word 'Batcave' even bizarrely became regarded as a subgenre of gothic music. The deathrock revival spread across the continent. In Spain, Quidam might have been kicking around since 1995 but they grasped the revival with both hands and finally released their debut *Barking, Mewing, Hissing & Mocking* in the summer of 2005. There were regular parties and events across the country and H Zombie also joined in with his side-project Naughty Zombies, while Portugal had its very own Graveyard Sessions. In Italy, gothabillies Scarlet And The Spooky Spiders kicked off around 2003 with Date At Midnight following four years later. In Denmark,

(((S)))'s progressive art-rock slotted into the outskirts of the scene, while there was an even bigger explosion out in Germany with bands like Bloody Dead And Sexy, the reformed Murder At The Registry and Zadera. A new indie record label called Strobelight embraced the genre as did specialist clubs such as Under Cover Of Darkness and Pagan Love Songs, named after the Virgin Prunes single and run by brothers Ralf and Thomas Thyssen (the latter of whom is now editor of Germany's *Gothic* magazine), not to mention the countless 'pogo parties' that became the next big thing. Given how quickly the German scene had apparently been progressing away from the old school sound, these deathrock and 'Batcave' events provided an arena for those bands with a more traditional sound to be heard. Torchbearers The House Of Usher and the now defunct The Merry Thoughts were played back-to-back with British bands like Voices Of Masada and Vendemmian in a scene which pretty much became the under-underground of German gothic.

As testament to the changing face of goth within Eastern Europe, New York's Drop Dead deathrock festival relocated first to Prague then Lisbon and was moved to Vilnius in Lithuania in 2010. Each time, it has been supported by a mixture of local and touring bands not to mention copious amounts of hairspray!

Even so, things remained underground as Lithuanian Konstantin remembers: "My first alternative gig was around 2003 and I was amazed because I never realised there were so many goths in my city ... You would never see anyone looking alternative during the day because there was a really low level of tolerance among the general public, so instead alternative people moved in their own small circles and they used to rent houses outside the city to throw little parties. There were different scenes but they never used to mix. For example, you would never see a goth drinking with a metalhead, or a punk with a skinhead – it was like a small war! There were a couple of events that were called Underground Unite that pulled all the different alternative communities together but usually it lasted only for a week. Things then gradually changed as the numbers got smaller and the different subcultures started to mix a few years later. The main problem was poverty – it was the same in Latvia and Estonia."

Bands in the UK took a much more humorous

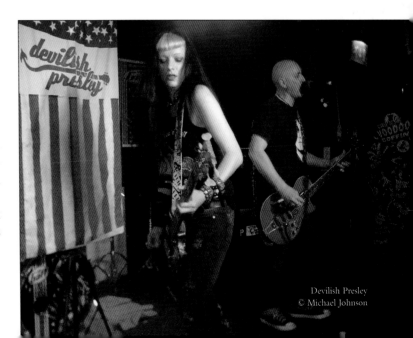

Devilish Presley
© Michael Johnson

approach to the deathrock style with Zombina And The Skeletones, Uninvited Guest, The Scary Bitches, garage rock band Devilish Presley and an early version of Screaming Banshee Aircrew coming under its umbrella. It even spread to Japan with 13th Moon and the more Misfits-styled Balzac. Interestingly, the scene's originators Christian Death and 45 Grave have both gone back to their metal roots with a new and much heavier sound which is quite the opposite of what those more contemporary acts are trying to create.

But the new wave of American deathrock tried to keep away from its metal and even glam roots. Michael 'Uncle Nemesis' Johnson: "The interesting thing is, our hypothetical Batcaver might not even feel at home in a present-day deathrock club. That might seem strange since today's deathrock scene is in many ways the inheritor of the Batcave spirit. But it's so stylised these days, in a way it never was in the early '80s – when, after all, it was all so new that the [gothic] style hadn't even been invented. People assume that everyone at the Batcave looked like Jonny Slut. In fact, there was only one person at the Batcave who looked like Jonny Slut, and that was Jonny Slut!" he says, referring to the keyboardist from Specimen's trademark messy mohawk, tops made from fishnets and distinctive spidery eye make-up. He continues: "[But] as I observed when Specimen played at the Wave Gotik Treffen [in 2009], the contrast between the band's look and the fans' look is quite telling: Specimen are the originals, the inventors. They don't follow the present-day style code." And the present-day Batcave style code seems to be hugely inspired

Kommunity FK as they are today.
© Michael Johnson

by Jonny Slut's unique image from the 1980s. Patrik Mata from original deathrock band Kommunity FK has also noticed the visual differences between the old and new movements: "As far as looking incredible [is concerned] there are now thousands of online clothing shops [and] designers … Although there seems to be a lot of lookalikes nowadays, there are a few whom appear to be trying to find their originality. Anything goes and everything is possible, which does not surprise me one bit." He adds, laughing: "It's 'cool' to be goth! Vampires with a six-pack, vampire films with shite soundtracks … it's kind of funny to see the rich Hollywood stars dressing in all black these days! Black nail polish, black suits and dresses – I bet that they don't know or even give a fuck as to where this fashion comes from!"

The new American deathrock: Christ Vs Warhol © Christ Vs Warhol.

While the revived deathrock look is still popular out in Europe and new bands are still being born – Christ Vs Warhol and Fangs On Fur are two of the more recent ones from the US – its music has also been assimilated into a more theatrical experience that played on dark cabaret. Paris' Katzenjammer Kabarett, The Dresden Dolls, Deadfly Ensemble (featuring Cinema Strange's Lucas Lanthier as well as Marzia Rangel and Steven James from Christ Vs Warhol) and Frank The Baptist – all from the US, although the latter has since relocated to Germany – played on this not only through their look but also through their dramatic music and performance. This created yet another cross-over genre that was not only true to goth's post-punk roots but also helped bring in interest from outside the scene too. "I think the Deadfly Ensemble was a perfect continuation [of what I was doing before]," Lucas Lanthier explains. "People often associate me with the first Cinema Strange album and forget, or are simply unaware, that there have been several albums since then, all forging ahead into hopefully at least a little bit of new territory. When the whole discography, including the Deadfly Ensemble albums, is taken into account, I think that there is a fairly smooth continuum with no really wild detours. Since the beginning, it's been about storytelling songs and their dramatic presentation."

The deathrock and horror punk styles have also helped bring back goth's shady association with vampires. A lot of the disassociation that took place in the '90s seems to have been mostly eroded due to the mainstream popularity

Horror jewellery and a rockabilly dress at the Wave
Gotik Treffen.
© Stephen Milward

of *Twilight* and *True Blood* and bands like The 69 Eyes, who play up to their Helsinki Vampires tag on a regular basis. Now it's done knowingly within the more developed goth scenes with a tongue more firmly in cheek, so it isn't perceived as too serious. However vampire culture is a bit more mainstream these days and aimed less directly at a gothic audience, which is no longer perceived as a youth culture. Unlike the '80s Brat Pack cool of *The Lost Boys,* the '90s erotica of *Interview With The Vampire* and *Bram Stocker's Dracula* or the more contemporary slickness of *Blade* – all of which appealed more directly to the underground goth scenes through wardrobes and soundtracks – the *Twilight Saga* itself is perceived as being a bit too trendy by most goths despite a cameo role from gothfather Peter Murphy in the third instalment *Eclipse*. But like gothic metal, the prolific film franchise based on Stephenie Meyer's vampire books has revived an interest in gothic fashion worldwide and encouraged high street stores to stock horror themed and lacey clothing and accessories.

In the more recent scenes, like those in India and Egypt, vampire culture seems to play a more literal role with many assuming that it's a relevant part of the gothic subculture rather than just a metaphorical one. A lot of this misinterpretation could be partly due to the underground goth scene keeping itself to itself, even online, thus more dramatic interpretations of the movement are easier to find by those seeking more information. It's similar to the UK media focusing on the strangest, most controversial creatures they could find and labelling them gothic because they were far more shocking and interesting to the public than the real, more passive movement.

Just as the flamboyancy of the '80s Batcave scene seemed to become little more than a fashion concept, deathrock seems in danger of doing much the same as the look is now so easy to put together off-the-peg, you can even buy ready-made mohawks and messier deathhawks. Former Christian Death keyboard player Gitane Demone opines: "Goth came out of deathrock in a more flouncy, less punk-driven way, in looks and music." But now in Germany, deathrock is a distinct brand within the goth scene rather than the other way round and the Jonny Slut look is almost a uniform. Even Clan Of Xymox's Ronny Moorings has noticed a shift in perception over the years: "Goth is a subculture again but also more a fashionable one. It is not really all about the music anymore but also clothing; showing your latest outfit and being seen. There's an appeal for kids to become 'gothic' so they can rebel against their parents or schoolmates or whatever. But I welcome it because I think there are too many boring people around and this will give it some diversion!"

With this in mind, it seems rather appropriate that a gothic craze based pretty much exclusively around fashion has been developing in New York. 'Gucci Goth' was a label chosen by former Brooklyn goth-cum-DJ Daniel

UK tattoo artist and model Rachael Huntington,
make-up: Krystel Gohel; clothing: Jane Doe Latex
© silent-view.com

Dodecahedron to encourage young blood into new music that had a dark edge but wasn't actually part of the goth scene *per se*. "After spending time around the people, the clubs [and] the bands, I came to realise that goth in its 'real' form is either '80s nostalgia worship or bad techno nights," he explains. "It's not fashionable and outside of ever-shrinking 'parents-suck-I'm-so-edgy' circles, it's not cool or appealing to young people … if anything, most people view it as cheesy. But there's a whole scene right now of new bands and artsy people wearing black and putting on nights with weird music [yet they] also embrace pop culture and fashion. It's almost totally disconnected from the 'real' goth scene but it's far more vibrant and happening. That's why the motto of Gucci Goth is 'Fake Goth is the Real Goth'."

As a concept, the idea of finding 'goth' in trendier, more unsuspecting places might have been around for some time – arguably it was rife back in the days when ready-made gothwear wasn't an option and outfits would be pieced together from whatever black items could be found. But the name is very new.

Dodecahedron, who recently moved to Berlin, has even set up a Facebook group and various blogs dedicated to the subject and he seems to have tapped into something that takes the trendier ideals of the current Shoreditch scene and turns them up to 11. Gucci Goth is about current pop trends like house music and R&B and talks about the gothic style that the likes of Rihanna, Lady Ga Ga and Christina Aguilera embrace in their videos with designer couture and plenty of (gold) bling. Fashion-wise, it's the modern equivalent of Zandra Rhodes' designer punk creations and it's also perhaps the kind of style that the original punk scene would have taken a blow torch to, but the DJ and blogger reckons

The latest craze to hit the US: it's Gucci Goth!
© Daniel Dodecahedron

this new faction revives the whole 'scene', pushing it forward and making it more real: "[Old school goth] was just kids dressing up and partying at clubs and somehow it spun out into this thirty-plus year subculture with giant festivals, sub-groups, even [Renaissance] Fair connections ... 'Real' goth lost the craziness and the originality and just became about a dress code ... Rather than rejecting the mainstream, Gucci Goth embraces it, paints it with a darker veneer and incorporates it into itself ... [It's] mainly about keeping it real rather than adhering to a dress code."

With Gucci Goth comes the new musical subgenre 'witch house' and its wonderfully-named sister 'gravewave'. They're often defined as a type of electronic shoegaze or, as Michael Johnson puts it: "like a Blair Witch Project take on ambient trance, or no-wave electronica as produced by Dario Argento." Dodecahedron himself describes it as: "the black shroud covering the corpse of the previous year's obsession with beach-pop and chillwave." Bands include S4LEM (whose music graced the runways at fashion house Givenchy's Spring/Summer 2011 show), White Ring and GR†LLGR†LL. Zola Jesus and Former Ghosts also fit into the category with their lo-fi yet contemporary takes on gothic dreampop and even dark-edged hip-hop is welcome – Canadian duo The Weeknd and Philly rapper Santigold have both sampled songs from Siouxsie And The Banshees' 1980 album *Kaleidoscope* on recent hit singles.

While not quite fitting with the witch house genre, there's also some Gucci Goth crossover with Canadian post-industrial act Dandi Wind's Fan Death project, and London-based band The xx, who seem to have had more success Stateside than in their own country with their songs being used on fashion runways and TV show *Grey's Anatomy*. Singer Romy Madley Croft recently

Lady Amaranth © Taya Uddin

guested with NYC Witch House/dubstep duo Creep on the single 'Days'.

In Isolation's Ryan Swift has been watching the new trend with interest. "I would actually say that dark music is at an even higher plateau in the UK at the moment," he says. "You've got bands appearing and visiting like Zola Jesus, Esben And The Witch, Anna Calvi, Effi Briest – all with a hugely dark edge to them and yet still getting critical acclaim. Even [the] less-extreme 'dark edge' bands are having success… Chapel Club's debut album [recently] hit number 16 in the 'real' charts, and The Joy Formidable are touring and selling out large venues around the country. If goth bands think they've got what it takes, now really is the time." He adds with a wink: "Just don't tell 'em you're a goth!"

GOTHIK ÜBER ALLES

It's almost a case of things coming back into fashion if you wait long enough, but as promising as the latest developments could be, this newly emerged dark scene hasn't quite spread to the rest of the world yet. A good example is the Scandinavian goth market, which is still very much ensconced in either the metal-hybrid or more electro-heavy music. Jorgen from Sweden's Dr Arthur

Dark Mort modelling items by Swedish designer Veil Of Visions.
© Taya Uddin

Krause tried to set up the Gothenburg Gothic Gathering for those into the more traditional sound but after several gigs, it has seemingly stuttered. "I'm sorry to say there is no goth scene worth the name any more and there isn't a large enough audience to make a [traditional gothic rock] band popular," he says. "There are still a few fans that come to our concerts but the younger people are more interested in gothic

The Birthday Massacre
© Dependent Records

metal. Bands like Deathstars and Tiamat are far away from what we are doing."

From the more teenage-orientated gothic metal scene, there arose another youth movement that the media tried to label as the new goth: emo. Originally an emotional offshoot of punk, a darker looking version became mislabelled as goth during the early 2000s with former hardcore bands My Chemical Romance, AFI and Aiden being especially popular. The mainstream media latched onto their black clothing, dyed hair and make-up, referring to them as either goth or emo depending on the mood of the day. Now Scotland has its very own version, what the Glasgow Survival website refers to as "The Schemo – a neddy goth"! Actually, both AFI and Aiden actually crossed over with the real goth scene through respective dark electronic side-projects Blaqk Audio and William Control. Both projects gained moderate interest in the underground scene on opposite sides of the Atlantic even if they received little publicity for them. Aiden's Wil Francis has name-checked Depeche Mode's uber-dark *Violator* as a huge influence on his solo material, while AFI's Davey Havok got tattooed with VNV Nation's logo. He even hired in the services of Ronan Harris from the band to help with programming on the single 'Miss Murder'.

The emo craze also overlapped a little with what New York electro-industrial punks Mindless Self Indulgence and Toronto's The Birthday Massacre were doing, both of whom were initially signed to the underground label Metropolis. While MSI hired in the services of spooky artist Jhonen Vasquez to design their album artwork, The Birthday Massacre's sugar-coated

Maria from Finnish band Beati Mortui
© Danse Macabre

dark pop crossed over between scenes while singer Chibi's gothic lolita-inspired style meant the band shared some of Emilie Autumn's dedicated fanbase. In fact, the Canadian goth scene as a whole has undergone quite a transformation recently with established bands like Rhea's Obsession and the one-time gothabillies Vampire Beach Babes adopting a very different sound. More electronic acts like Ayria and Montreal's industrial Rise Of The Fallen have also made a mark on the scene and signified a definite change in musical direction compared its new wave roots.

A small but healthy underground goth scene still continues to thrive in Finland, mostly around Helsinki and Tampere with clubs, shops, bands and the four-day Lumos festival providing suitable entertainment for the darkly-inclined. Groups such as Sinmasters (a Two Witches electronic side-project), Silent Scream and Beati Mortui are among the better-known bands in the scene there, both of whom regularly play throughout Europe. In Iceland, small underground scenes have existed in Reykjavík in the past but without the specialist clubs or venues, these days it's more a case of wearing black and listening to music with friends. The darker sounds of local post-rock/indie bands like Sigur Rós have almost allowed gothic influence to seep unwittingly into more mainstream music there.

Over the last decade, Germany's Schwarze Szene has become a mighty force to be reckoned with and market research suggests there are currently around 150,000 self-proclaimed goths there alone. But still there are those who continue to dismiss it. Its impact has been felt outside the borders with export band Rammstein becoming infamous around the world for their, quite literally, explosive live arena shows. Former Neue Deutsche Härte act Unheilig went from topping Germany's alternative DAC charts to enjoying success in the mainstream hit parade, something that naturally earned them accusations of selling out among followers of the more underground gothic scene. "Every time you switch on the TV, he's there," explains Artwork's Jochen Schoberth.

"He's even on the judges panel for our version of *X-Factor*!" But those defending Unheilig simply suggest that they have helped make goth and the Schwarze Szene more acceptable in German culture and helped clothing and lifestyle companies expand. In fact several of the country's gothic clothing brands now frequently sponsor events and use well-known dark scene bands to endorse their edgy attire.

"In Germany, the music is more modern in general," says Slimelight DJ Steve Weeks who regularly travels the continent to spin guest slots at European clubs. "I've never heard lots of old '80s UK goth played for example [and] a lot of the old German standards were not scene hits in the UK. Most of the current German guitar-based gothic acts (like Unheilig) don't seem to be well known here and they don't mimic the UK sound." Attempts have been made to bring these bands over to the UK but their very German sound just doesn't seem to travel so well, despite the popularity of Rammstein.

And of those other industrial cross-over bands, the mittelalter scene's heavier components have been gradually trying to cross over with the UK metal scene. Subway To Sally and In Extremo have already made attempts and no doubt others will be on their heels. As a large number of goths focus on more elaborate outfits these days, mittelalter comfortably fits with the re-enactment scene that went one step further than RPG-ing and seems to have replaced Pagan moots in the gothic calendar.

Arguably such fancy dress parades are a million miles away from goth's post-punk roots, which were all about being true to yourself and making a stand but then again, it's not so different from those anarchic punks of the 1970s that regarded the Sex Pistols as poseurs. If goth has become more of a

Unheilig live © Per Ake Warn

fashion statement than a musical style these days, then those recycled gothic fashions in the high street and on the catwalks still play an important role in raising interest in the dark scene that lurks behind them.

Artist Anne Sudworth muses: "Goth has become much more acceptable, though it remains an underground scene and one that many still describe as extreme. More people have become part of it and obviously, they might have a different attitude to the scene than those who came to it earlier on. Everything evolves as society evolves [and] the society we live in now is very different from the one when goth started. Now the goth scene is made up of a much wider age group and is much more diverse, with many smaller groups branching off into other directions …"

The gothic and dark metal scenes – incorporating industrial metal and symphonic – are now far bigger than the real underground goth movement. With such a high profile out in mainland Europe, it's already showing signs of engulfing much of what was regarded as 'true goth' from the '80s and not just musically either as its less flouncy, more structured uniform has become popular dark attire. Not only is it more accessible but it also has a much bigger budget behind it so is more appealing to larger promoters and labels. Europe's dark calendar is now filled with additional events such as Amphi, the *Sonic Seducer*-run M'era Luna (which took over from the annual *Zillo* magazine alternative festivals in Hildesheim in 2000) and Belgium's Metal Female Voices and Waregem's Gothic, not to mention more specialist shows and club nights, often referred to as 'parties'. In the UK a new festival was debuted in York in 2010 called DV8 – it's the first event in this country to closely follow the European dark music festival format.

Just as UK Decay's Abbo intended it, goth has retained its ambiguous status and become a melting pot of fashion, music, lifestyle and cultural elements that all retain that dark

Cecile and Rebecca at Kensal Green Cemetery
© Martin Small

aesthetic while still managing to elude a more precise definition. Goth clubs around the world from Japan to the Czech Republic to Israel play music that is universally recognised as goth while its punters wear varying degrees of gothic dress. Its influence can be felt in the world of fashion and contemporary music, irrespective of any kind of publicity. "I think when you've got a combination of melancholy, art and sexuality, people will always be attracted to it," summarises Nightbreed's Trevor Bamford. "The gothic scene is like the world in microcosm, it's like a big umbrella in which trends will come and go."

Unlike other subcultures, goth has not only eluded definition but its followers have also been reluctant to be categorised. Whether connected with negative associations brought about by bad press or a simple stubbornness to be considered individual, new names and subgenres are constantly emerging. Just as darkwave, cold wave and witch house have caught on, so there's potential for the latest reinterpretations: 'rock noir' (coined by Italian dark band Belladonna) and 'trash vogue' (originally invented by Xris and Ed Banshee, formerly Screaming Banshee Aircrew).

And so this thing (sometimes) called 'goth' has grown from a tiny seed in the UK and blossomed into the rarest and most unexpected flower. Goth may mean different things to different people and represent many alternative ideals in other countries but the fact that it continues to flourish as a creative subculture after all these years is testament to its common voice. This is the subculture that quite simply refuses to die!

APPENDIX: THE EVOLUTION OF GOTH STYLE

Think of 'Goth' and a snapshot of someone dressed in black with long, dyed hair and heavy make-up will probably come to mind but when the first gothic bands started to emerge in the late 1970s, their style was fairly casual. It simply revolved around shirts and jeans in dark colours so as not to show up the dirt. The Damned, Killing Joke, Siouxsie And The Banshees and Bauhaus were among those who favoured a more theatrical look, merging fancy dress items with glam and punk staples, like leather and the occasional item of fetishwear which still carried an aggressive and shocking message. Make-up was used not to enhance features but as a form of war paint worn by both sexes, a theme continued by the more image-aware Specimen, Alien Sex Fiend and Sex Gang Children. In retrospect, Specimen's glamorous keyboard player Jonny Slut's ripped fishnets and mohawk look is now regarded as an example of '80s gothic fashion despite him having a very unique appearance at the time!

But what has come to be referred to as 'the gothic look' was one originally worn by bands as a type of stage wear and wasn't picked up as a fashion trend until much later. The Sisters Of Mercy popularised long hair and aviator shades, worn with lots of black leather for a polished biker look, while The Cult went from Native American Indian jewellery and head-dresses to long, black locks and pirate shirts before moving onto leather and cowboy hats. Along with The Mission's dandyish image and the Fields Of The Nephilm's Wild West chic, these looks were quickly copied by fans and filtered through into high street fashions where the classic rebellious look of t-shirt, jeans and a leather jacket was given a modern black-wash with added fringing and decorative badges. Siouxsie Sioux and Patricia Morrison's striking vampish looks remain just as iconic as they were back in the day despite both ladies changing their appearances in more recent times. Without them, it's unlikely that big, black back-combed hair, corsets, costume jewellery and lace would have made an appearance into the gothic wardrobe.

The application of the word 'goth' played a huge part in bringing the sound and look in a more macabre and Victorian mourning direction, which moved things further away from the movement's punk roots. It also helped create interest in what was now a movement with a lasting appeal. Goth shifted from simply being an extension of punk to a subculture in its own right that carried a very dark aesthetic.

The assimilation of different musical genres in the 1990s brought their own fashion cues. Electronic styles meshed with rave culture to create the brightly-coloured cybergoth that took a huge amount of influence not from bands but from Japanese anime and futuristic films. Synthetic fabrics, accessories made from bits of technology and plastic materials woven into unnaturally coloured hair made this almost an extension of the vibrant peacock punks from the 1970s and the military-themed outfits worn by rivet heads and industrial fans provided a more subdued alternative. On the flip-side, the gothic metal subgenre continued the black leather and vampiric cues that gothic rock had flirted with a decade earlier and mixed them with Hollywood's own reinterpretations.

The contemporary gothic look has come a long way from such humble beginnings. From the gothic lolita style made popular by Japanese visual kei bands to the rockabilly pin-up, steampunk and flamboyant modern deathrocker, goth's wardrobe has expanded moving away from the traditional black and towards colour and mass-produced styles. The traditional gothic look from the '80s has been replaced by a more ornate style with luxurious, often expensive, fabrics and attention to historical detail. What began as a DIY fashion worn by bands to make a statement has now turned designer, inspiring catwalk collections and haute couture, as demonstrated by the new Gucci Goth tag. It's rather fitting that for many, goth is now more about fashion than music or social change and it continues to communicate globally through its striking image to this day.

(c) Lip Service clothing

The following people were interviewed by the author for this book: Michelle Archer (Brigandage); Michael 'Uncle Nemesis' Johnson; Nik and Mrs Fiend (Alien Sex Fiend); Per-Ake Warn ; Si Denbigh (March Violets); Roger 'Trotwood' Nowell (Skeletal Family); Andy Heintz; Stephane Lord; Erika Grapes; Ryan Swift; Ralf Epke; Rosi 'Rosalie' Uwins; Anne Sudworth; Garry Hornby; Max Flowers; Sebastian Rizza; Steve Weeks; Vx 69 (Punish Yourself); Neville Cope; Ingela Lordsdotter; Tracey Gibson; Lauryn Malott; Nina Rieser; Matthew North; Ruby Soho; Chandrika Maria; Maurice Grunbaum; Mick Mercer; Szelevényi Gellért; Siouxsie Sioux; 'Cadavre Exquis'; Graf Starkall; Daniela Barría Segovia; Daniel Dodecahedron; Farzana Fiaz; DJ Ørlög; Louis Chambers; Mark Rimmell; Chris Octavenomur; Konstantin Artamonov; Mortiis Ellefsen; Greg Mackintosh; Jen Vee Ibrahim; Yair Abelson; Hilla Bernstein; Hans Miniar Jónsson; Tamsin Margaret-Nita Rogers; Somi Arian; Raymond John Ross; Trevor Bamford; John F Keenan; Jon Klein; Martin 'Oldgoth' Coles; Neville Cope; Jamie Nova; Roger O'Donnell; Emilie Autumn; Christian Riou; Dinah Cancer; Gitane Demone; Patrik Mata; Suzuky Kawasaky; Kiwamu (Blood); Kaoru (Dir En Grey); Dynamite Tommy; Eric Burton; Jochen Schoberth; Luca Appennini (DJ BMC); Andreas Larsson; Kimmo Kuokka; Santeri Ihalainen 'Santuu'; Kevin Preece; Lucas Lanthier; Ryan Clark; Coffin Joe; Alun Hughes; Julie Kiss; Norbert Uzseka ; Jyrki Witch; Jyrki 69; Jorgen (Dr Arthur Krause); Lee 'chaos' Hodder; Ronny Moorings; Kevin 'Ogre' Ogilvie; Steve 'Abbo' Abbot; Karl 'Zoog' (Angelspit); Ezechiel (Sanctuary.cz); Drew Bernstein; Audrey Desprats-Colonna; Pat Hawkes-Reed; Tony Pettitt (Fields of the Nephilim); Hein Frode Hansen; Marloes Bontje; DJ DE'Ath; Nadir Amrioui; Alea Der Bescheidene; Monica Richards; Tilo Wolff ; Wil Francis (Aiden/William Control); Davey Havok (AFI/Blaqk Audio); Mark Rowe; Stephen Milward.

Every effort has been made to correctly credit the photographers' material used within these pages. The publisher would be grateful if any errors were brought to their attention so the matter can be rectified in future editions.